Keep Going:
A 30-Day Devotional
of Encouragement and
Truth for Moms

Jessica Fraser

Scripture taken from the English Standard Version®. Copyright ©2001
by Crossway. Used by permission. All rights reserved.

ISBN: 9781712606100

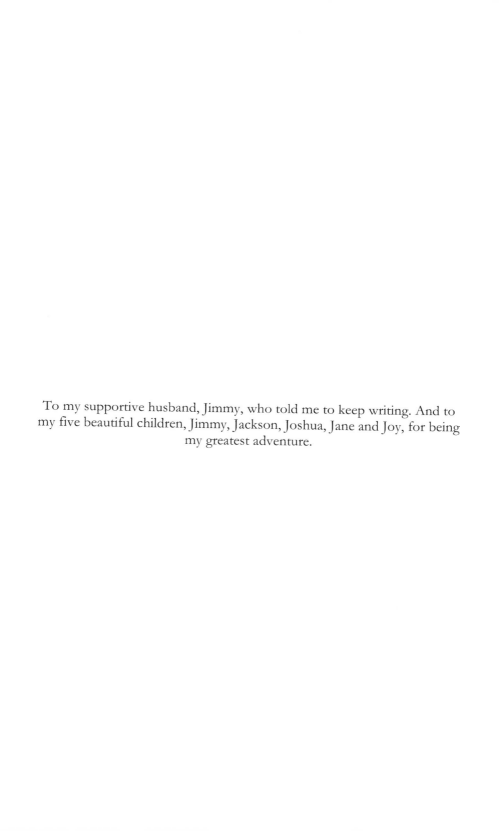

To my supportive husband, Jimmy, who told me to keep writing. And to my five beautiful children, Jimmy, Jackson, Joshua, Jane and Joy, for being my greatest adventure.

CONTENTS

INTRODUCTION

I first published a book in second grade. Bound between two pieces of laminated construction paper, *The Beautiful Field* followed a dog desperate to change the world. Missy, the main character, was surrounded by litter and searched for a way to save the earth. I dedicated the book to all dogs killed by pollution.

It was a profound message for a second grader.

All these years later, I've written words with the intent of sending an even more powerful message to a generation parched for its life-giving truth: God is exactly who He says He is.

This 30-day devotional took years to write. I wrote it in the margins of motherhood, through the highs and the lows. I wrote in the early hours of the morning between feedings and during naptime in the afternoons. I wrote it when I was exhausted yet joyful, hurt yet hopeful. It is a compilation of my stories as a mother, wife, daughter, sister and friend. These stories are not manufactured or fiction; they are part of the fiber of my memories. To let you in to read them is both exciting and terrifying because to make oneself vulnerable before others is difficult.

Each story in this book aims to point you back to Jesus. Maybe you'll laugh or cry as you read along, but the purpose is to give God the glory in all seasons and circumstances. I toiled away at putting these 30 devotionals together, constantly leaning on Scripture and prayer to guide me as I wrote and edited. I also received permission from my children and husband to share the stories you'll read. I read them out loud around the kitchen table, explaining to each member of my family I wanted them to feel comfortable with what is shared in this book. While names are not used, sometimes my kids wanted me to point out it was the "third son" or "my oldest." These 30 stories are just as much their stories as they are mine.

My hope, as a follower of Jesus, is for women to know their Bibles and be equipped to face the battle the world wages with us. "For we do not wrestle against flesh and blood, but against the rulers, against the authorities, against the cosmic powers over the present darkness, against the spiritual forces of evil in the heavenly places" (Ephesians 6:12). Sisters, we have to boldly be able to name our enemy in order to battle against him. Our enemy is the devil himself. The world is his playground and his darkness continues to spread.

Armed with Scripture and the unshakeable knowledge of who God is, we can change the course of history. We can be the ones who help turn the tide.

This devotional serves as a part of your arsenal against the enemy. Not only within the stories will you find Scripture and truth, but this book aims to further your walk with Jesus.

I've included a song recommendation to accompany each day's devotional. By the end of these readings, you will have a playlist of 30 of my favorite worship songs (and hopefully a few you haven't heard before). My prayer is, as you listen to the songs later, you'll be reminded of how God worked in your life as you studied His Word through this book.

I've also included for each day a section called, "How's my heart today?" One of my favorite things to ask people is the spiritual and emotional condition of their hearts. I'm not interested in the polite, "How are you?" I want to know the depths of your heart and where you're struggling or singing praises. I want to know the areas where God is working. Take this question seriously and be honest with your answers. This devotional isn't intended to be a coffee table book; it can become a journal of life change. Write down how you feel each day as a way of remembering what is going on in this season during the 30 days you're reading. Watch how God can transform you.

Next is a section called "Attitude of gratitude." Every night at our dinner table, our whole family shares one high point of the day, one low point and then one attitude of gratitude moment. This is a perspective shift for us. We want to acknowledge both the good and the hard in our days, but we never want to lose focus of thankfulness. Our God is the giver of good and perfect gifts (James 1:17), and one of those gifts was His Son. Focusing on gratitude in the midst of our daily lives puts our hearts in a posture of worship. For all God has done for us, we recognize Him and give thanks. This is our attitude of gratitude. You can write down one (or more!) things you're thankful for each day in this section.

Finally, there's a section called "Keep going." This is my signature phrase. I tell everyone I know as they run their race with Jesus to **keep going**. Keep going when it's hard. Keep going when it seems easy. Keep going when you're living in the tension of joy and grief at the same time. Keep going and keep pursuing the heart of

God. This section aims to take you further into your time with Jesus, digging deeper into His Word. While Scripture is associated within the stories, this area is the one designated to get you sitting with Jesus and hopefully looking at Scripture in a new light. Feel free to write down observations you have while reading in this devotional. Again, this isn't meant to be a coffee table book. This book is meant to travel with you over a 30-day period when God does a new, exciting work on your heart. Some days that work may be hard and others you may feel great freedom and release.

This devotional does not have parameters or guidelines. You are not bound by a rule you must do one devotional every day for 30 days. These 30 days were once only mine, sitting on the hard drive of my computer. Now, sister, they are yours. Feel the freedom to read them as you see fit. Share them with a friend. Find time to rest. Find time to dig deeper into Scripture. Ask questions. Write poems. As a follower of Jesus Christ, I think it is my duty to give away the gifts He has so freely given me. This book is one of those.

I pray this book finds you in a season where you surrender your heart and pursue God with the same recklessness He pursues you. And when you're done reading, don't stop chasing after His heart. Keep going.

DAY ONE

Before piecing the devotionals for this book together, I rested from writing. Stretching these muscles again has been hard; while I have access to the vast library of words like everyone else, sometimes the words don't easily come. The muscles are weak and without tone. Weaving words together into stories that point to Jesus seems like a difficult task. But when Jesus calls, I've learned to answer.

I thought I'd start this book with a brief introduction of myself. It still humbles me to my core people take time out of their day to read words I've been entrusted to write. And as I pour out a sometimes funny, sometimes difficult, but always truthful and vulnerable, part of myself into the pages of this devotional, I want you to know a bit about the person writing them.

I'm a parent trying to figure out how to navigate the raising of human beings without losing them, my mind, or my sanity. I'm a parent at the foot of the cross every day asking forgiveness and begging for patience and wisdom. I'm a parent without a manual of how in the world this job is supposed to be done, instead turning to Jesus and truth-giving, encouragement-pouring community.

I'm a mother of five children (and one fur baby) and wife to my high school sweetheart. The question I'm asked the most when I'm out and about with my big brood is, "You know how this happens, right?"

I assure you; I do.

And along the parenting path God taught me some beautiful, hard, hilarious, and life-changing lessons. You're entrusting me enough to take a few minutes out of your day to get a little peek in and, hopefully, when you're done, your cup feels a little more full. Because while we may be different in the number of kids we parent or how we parent, there is a universal truth of parenting - we need Jesus to get through this.

These devotionals are stories from my life that will point you back to Him. I won't offer you parenting advice (I'm still figuring this gig out for myself), I (hopefully) won't preach at you, and I certainly won't leave you feeling alone. You aren't the only one walking the path you're walking. Parenting is best done in the presence of Jesus and Jesus-loving community. Can black and white words from a fellow sojourner be your community? At times, absolutely, because community is built on the understanding we're here to encourage and speak truth into each other's lives so we all look more like Jesus.

This parenting thing is hard work. But the load is lightened when we do it in community with people who are living out the same hardships and joys. With five kids, I've got a story for almost every season. And they are the stories I want to share with you in hopes of encouraging you and letting you see how Jesus is alive and working in every aspect of my journey.

What's the takeaway from this first devotional? **You are loved**. You are so immensely loved by the Author and Creator of life He wanted you to know it in an abundance of ways. One of those ways is this little book - words strung together to make sentences on pages that will magnify His steadfast love for you. Today and always, no one will know the depths of your heart as well as Jesus does. He knows the aches because He's felt them firsthand. He knows your joys because He's the source of them. And He knows the only thing you need to get through each day is to keep your eyes locked on Him as you run your race.

Sister, let's get running.

"Therefore, since we are surrounded by so great a cloud of witnesses, let us also lay aside every weight, and sin which clings so closely, and let us run with endurance the race that is set before us" (Hebrews 12:1).

Song: *Can't Outrun Your Love* by Ellie Holcomb

How's my heart today?

Attitude of gratitude:

Keep going: Hebrews 12 references Hebrews 11, which is known as the "Hall of Faith." Read Hebrews 11 and 12, remembering the leaders of faith who ran their race before you. Take time to research and understand their stories. Let them inspire you and encourage you as you run the race Jesus put before you.

God has a plan for every person, and our important task is to pray for our children and prepare them to do the work God has planned for them to do. Faith allows us to entrust our children to God.

DAY TWO

I'm not ashamed to admit some days it's easier to put my kids in the car and head to a drive-thru for dinner. Let's face it, some days it isn't necessarily easier, it's just if I have to spread one more glob of peanut butter across a piece of bread, I may scream.

After a long week, I decided we would eat dinner at Taco Cabana. In an effort to get my kids as excited about the excursion as I was (and in turn, avoid a "But we want peanut butter and jelly!" meltdown), I jumped around the living room with an overly excited tone shouting, "Who's excited for Taco Cabana? I'm excited for Taco Cabana!" By the divine intervention of God, my kids looked at me with the same degree of excitement and peaceably agreed it was a good idea. *Thank you, Jesus,* I thought with a sigh of relief. God is still on His throne performing miracles, and I consider the approval of my kids on anything I suggest one of those – especially when it comes to food. Moms everywhere understand the magnitude of this win.

Once at Taco Cabana, I ordered what I considered to be the healthy, smart choice - grilled chicken fajitas. My three-year-old opened his mouth and took his first bite, but his face cringed with disapproval. He chewed and forced himself to swallow. I asked him what was wrong with his fajita, and his eyes locked on mine.

"This *isn't* a taco banana," he sternly said. "I thought you said we were getting taco banana."

Misunderstandings surround us daily. As parents, we may struggle to understand our children who are learning how to communicate. We may misunderstand the cues of our spouse. And in a digital world, it's almost too easy to misunderstand the intent and tone behind words typed out via text, email or social media. The enemy wants us to feel misunderstood in hope we'll place our faith in the fleeting things of this world.

Rest easy, sister, because our God does not misunderstand us.

"O Lord, you have searched me and known me!
You know when I sit down and when I rise up;
you discern my thoughts from afar.
You search out my path and my lying down
and are acquainted with all my ways.
Even before a word is on my tongue,
behold, O Lord, you know it altogether" (Psalm 139:1-4).

How beautiful is this knowledge that while the world around us may be full of misunderstandings, our Creator never fails to understand every ounce of our being? Take refuge in the words of the psalmist writing heartfelt praises to a God who is unchanging and all-knowing. He knows the desires of your heart and the steps of your story. He is a God who is not overwhelmed when you fall short because He has already rescued you and called you His. This Creator, this Author and Perfecter of your faith, will never misunderstand you because He knows you best. With Him, you'll never get grilled chicken instead of a banana.

Song: *The Wick* by Housefires

How's my heart today?

Attitude of Gratitude:

Keep going: Read the entirety of Psalm 139. Allow it to fully sink in that God keeps His all-knowing gaze upon you, especially in the times when your heart cries out and you feel unseen and unheard. Pray Psalm 139 out loud to finish your quiet time.

DAY THREE

One evening while answering emails at the kitchen table, I glanced up the stairs after hearing the feet of toddlers trample through toys on the floor, signifying an escape from bed. My husband sat on the couch listening to music, seemingly oblivious to the playful sounds from upstairs. I paused for a moment and then returned to my task, silently praying the added playtime before bed would result in a little extra sleep in the morning.

My three-year-old repeatedly yelled "Mommy!" and "Come here!" over and over from upstairs. Hoping for the best yet bracing myself for the worst, I headed up to see the reason for the fuss.

Before I could fully turn the corner at the top of the stairs, I saw it. I saw colorful lines strewn about into designs that, to me, made no sense. It was the artwork of youth - messy, rough and honest. But this piece of art did not adorn paper, or even walls, but instead, the carpet.

My only reaction was to gasp. Loudly.

I then heard feet barreling up the stairs behind me, and in a futile attempt to shield my husband from the Jackson Pollock-esque artwork on our carpet, I lunged forward, down a few stairs, and covered his eyes. I'm not quite sure what I was thinking, seeing as he towered almost a foot taller than me. Without much effort, he removed my hands from his eyes, moved me aside and finished his trek to the second floor. His jaw dropped when he saw the artwork.

We stood together before an array of deep yellow, red and blue lines. The face of a smiling child looked on from the gate separating us. The artist was happy. He was proud. His artwork was beautiful and big, a direct expression of his personality. There was no shame, no guilt, no hint of regret on his face. To him, those lines had meaning. For Mom and Dad, those lines brought a spectrum of emotions; we were angry at his disobedience but strained to keep from smiling at the look of accomplishment he proudly wore. Before my husband and I could utter any words, the one who tried to warn me earlier confidently said, "It wasn't me, Mommy."

And it wasn't. The artist clenched in his tiny, pudgy hands the three markers that helped him complete his masterpiece. He smiled one more smile before dropping his markers, turning around and getting back into bed without a single word. (How he got access to those markers still baffles me to this day.)

Children can look at anything and think of it as a canvas; a blank piece of paper, the kitchen table, walls, and in this case, a clean carpet. With each blank canvas comes a new opportunity to share a bit of themselves. It's the messy scribblings of toddlers that reveal who they are, from the bold shades they choose to the canvas they adorn with their artwork.

But for God, we are the blank canvas. Isaiah 64:8 states, "But now, O Lord, you are our Father; we are the clay, and you are our potter; we are all the work of your hand."

We are the blank canvas in which God carefully reveals a part of Himself. And while we were created in His image, we are sinners. We are at times artwork we wish we could shield from other's eyes. There are moments as mothers when we lose our sense of holiness and become nothing more than voice-raising balls of frustration. But then we have an opportunity to give thanks in the hectic moments for His grace and mercy and allow our hearts to be re-molded by His almighty hand.

While motherhood is challenging, remember the Potter specifically molded you to be the mother you are. Offer up your heart as a blank canvas each day where God can do His holy work. God has specifically chosen you to mother your children, and I imagine

He's standing in heaven, clay and markers tightly in His grip, smiling at His beautiful creation.

Song: *Canvas and Clay* by Pat Barrett and Ben Smith

How's my heart today?

Attitude of Gratitude:

Keep going: Isaiah 64 is a gorgeous chapter of Scripture. Read it in its entirety through the lens that this awesome God took the time to delicately and intricately craft you. What do you need to remember about your identity in Jesus today?

DAY FOUR

My eyes stung as I fought back tears. Looking down at my daughter, just one week old, the warmth of her body overwhelmed me; the steady rise and fall of her chest and the breath released from between her slightly parted lips brought me both comfort and anxiety. Just two years prior I surrendered two unborn babies into the Father's arms. Even when holding my newborn in my arms, I felt the weight of fear in the wake of those losses.

Two years earlier, a stark white and sterile hallway greeted me before the sun broke the horizon. I walked slowly down the hall while doctors and nurses scrubbed their hands and forearms in preparation for surgery. I was quietly escorted into a room where I changed into my gown and awaited anesthesia. The pain was still so fresh, and I was hoping the medicine would help to numb it, to numb me. Because sometimes allowing ourselves to fully feel the weight of our trials can be the hardest part.

Nurses cycled through my room, walking me again and again through the procedure. It would be quick, and recovery would be too. But how long would the pain of knowing they were about to scrape away the remains of my child from my uterus last? How long would that recovery be?

Little was said before wheeling my gurney down the hall to the operating room. Each time I closed my eyes, I was back in the ultrasound room looking at a baby - my baby - who no longer had a heartbeat. And just a week prior, it was there. It was slow and steady, hanging on just barely, but the *thump thump thump* was there. This was the new reality. No baby would come home nestled in receiving blankets.

A few short months after the first surgery, I would miscarry again. Some did not understand my heartbreak because I already had three healthy children. Many offered kind words and prayers. I was urged to lean into God, but up until this point, I struggled with what that meant. How can I lean into God? What does that mean and what does it look like, especially when our hearts are broken? It is hard to feel His faithfulness when we feel emptied out inside.

I didn't want platitudes in the depths of this hurt. I wanted life change. I read Psalm 34:18 over and over, "The Lord is near to the brokenhearted and saves the crushed in spirit." Scripture began to transform me. I realized leaning in would look like surrender. I would surrender my own control, anger, and confusion in order to receive the Lord's comfort. Scripture revealed itself to me in new ways and I began to rejoice through my trial. I rejoiced not for the loss of two children, but for the victory through Jesus that I would one day hold them in heaven.

A few months later, my oldest son, only five at the time, bounded down the stairs and into my room. He shook my arm until I woke up.

"Mom, I had a dream and God told me we were going to have a baby!" His face was aglow. His heart hopeful. I mustered a simple smile, unsure how to respond because we were not trying to conceive.

A few days later, a pregnancy test revealed his dream to be true.

As I looked down at my daughter, just a few short years after surrendering two unborn children directly to the Father's arms, I didn't try to push back the memories of loss. I was thankful for the steadfast love my Heavenly Father showed me as He walked with me through the pain. I thanked Him for the vivid memory of the sound of heartbeats, in tandem with my own, that now beat in heaven.

God pours out His love for us in the same way we pour out our love for our children. Lean in when it's hard and you want to control the situation. Lean in when you aren't quite sure what the outcome will be. Lean in when all you want to do is run. Because if you lean in and surrender, you'll find yourself wrapped in the arms of a Father who loves you so much He'll never let you go.

Song: *Death was Arrested* by North Point Worship

How's my heart today?

Attitude of gratitude:

Keep going: The Gospel of Matthew frequently references the Old Testament. Matthew's purpose of writing was to convince the Jews that Jesus was the Messiah they long hoped for, and in referencing the Old Testament, he was connecting the dots between the prophecy of the Messiah and Jesus Himself. Visit Matthew 5:1-12. This part of Jesus' Sermon on the Mount was titled "The Beatitudes." Beatitudes are a state of great joy or overwhelming blessing. Jesus listed blessings here. Which do you struggle to understand and receive? Why?

DAY FIVE

My husband and I are in the business of raising children, and unfortunately for our home (specifically our yard), that means it takes a back seat. While away on vacation over the summer, the dry Texas heat got its footing and wreaked havoc on our grass. Chinch bugs moved in and ate our entire front yard all the way to the roots, leaving behind only dead remains. When the rains came, our neighbors' yards flourished. Ours stuck out like a brown, dead sore thumb.

After a few months of embarrassment and frustration, we decided it was time to re-sod. We waited until the heat officially broke, and we set aside one day of a long weekend to tackle the project. I figured it would take approximately two hours. Maximum. My husband would pick up the grass and soil, we would enlist our mighty team of able-bodied children, and we'd be done before the first Saturday morning college football kickoff.

Obviously, an understanding of how to keep my yard alive isn't the only place I struggle.

Six hours later we weren't finished. Eight hours later we weren't finished. When we started the task some of our lovely neighbors came out to offer advice. One man, well-versed in yard care, offered to rent an aerator with us because, as he put it, "you can't lay sod without aerating first."

Ten hours, one aerator, one trunkful of soil and half a pallet of grass later, our yard still wasn't done. We were half a pallet of grass short and the store selling the grass was now closed. Our yard, once a dry wasteland of dead grass, was now half-complete and war-torn. I wanted to put a sign up that said, "Don't worry, we aren't finished yet."

A week later, we finally finished the yard.

I can tell time, but I've always struggled to accurately assess how long a project will take. My Type-A, let's-do-this-fast-and-move-on attitude always miscalculates. I think the yard or homework or trip to the grocery store will be quick and painless, and then a few hours later I'm pulling my hair out wondering how I so poorly mismanaged the whole thing.

I get my timing wrong when it comes to God too. I want to present Him with my prayers and then have them answered on the spot. I want the microwave outcome - put it in uncooked and a few minutes later it's ready to consume. I want God to operate on my timetable as I ask for healing or answers in hopes of immediately getting results.

But God has never operated on the timetable of His creation, because He is not bound by time as we are. We are created from the dust of the earth, and He is the beginning and the end; the One who always was and always will be. His timing to answer prayers or show His hand in a situation is not based on my urgency for Him to move. It's based solely on the sacred and holy method of His plans. I am bound by a period of time I want to bend to meet my needs, and God is bound in limitless time where He works all things for the good of His children **in His time.**

I think when Peter penned these words all those years ago, he was penning them for people just like me, "But do not overlook this one fact, beloved, that with the Lord one day is as a thousand years, and a thousand years as one day. The Lord is not slow to fulfill His promise as some count slowness, but is patient toward you" (2 Peter 3:8-9).

What I count as slowness, God counts as time to fulfill His promise.

When I squirm and throw tantrums that I want answers sooner, He remains patient.

God's timing is not my timing and thank God for that.

14

I am my front yard. I have to die daily to my personal desires and then be aerated, sprinkled with good soil for seeds, and re-sodded. And it won't take two hours. Or even 10. It will take as long as God needs to fulfill His plans and promises for my life.

Sister, whatever your heart is crying out for today, rest it at the feet of the cross and then rest in the assurance God's timing will not fail you. It won't forget you. It won't overlook you. His promise will be fulfilled, and His patience won't wear out. He weeps when you weep and laughs when you laugh. His joy is your own. Let the foundation of your heart abandon the hopes of time bound by human constraints and instead open it up to the Lord for the mighty work He wants to do.

Again, God's timing is not our timing and thank God for that.

Song: *Reckless Love* by Cory Asbury

How's my heart today?

Attitude of gratitude:

Keep going: Jesus spoke about God's timing. Read Matthew 24:36-51 and Acts 1:1-11. There are mysteries of God we are not designed to understand. But our faith can propel us through. Whatever prayer you have brought before God that feels unanswered, whatever season that feels distant from Him, know His timing is perfect. It is not an empty promise. How can you change the way you pray knowing, in faith, God's timing is better than your own?

DAY SIX

My kids love to find new ways to embarrass me.

A few years back, three of my children were attending preschool at the same time. We arrived early for school with the usual group of moms who share our same affinity for extreme punctuality. I chugged a cup of coffee in the car, and upon arrival to the school I found myself doing the potty dance. I brought the three boys into the restroom with me and asked them to wait patiently by the sinks.

The boys did as they were told. When I was finished going potty, I washed my hands. The door to the restroom opened and a familiar face walked in. As she greeted us with her warm smile, my oldest spoke up.

"My mom just pooped," he said confidently. "In that one." His little chubby hand pointed to the stall where the toilet I used was still flushing. My face, at the same moment, flushed a shade of red I didn't know was humanly possible.

"No! I didn't! I only..." my words trailed off as I tried to regain some sort of dignity.

"It's ok," the mom interjected. "We all poop." She smiled a big, genuine smile and then closed the stall door behind her.

"But...no...I...didn't..." I stuttered, looking more guilty than truthful at this point. My case was lost based on the evidence I couldn't defend myself. I was an innocent woman wrongly convicted. Three little faces looked up at me with grins so big I was scared they may freeze that way. Embarrassed and flustered, I hurried them out of the bathroom, and they snickered all the way to class sign-ins.

I figured a devotional was a good place to finally defend myself: I didn't poop that morning. And that's the truth.

To this day, I'm mortified to take any of my children into a restroom with me in fear I'll be wrongly accused of restroom behaviors I didn't do. But despite my embarrassment, I'm thankful for laughter - even if it is at my expense.

In Ecclesiastes 3:4 Solomon writes there is a "time to weep, and a time to laugh." When God created us in His holy image, laughter was part of that. God knew it would stimulate the heart, increase endorphins released to the brain, soothe tension and even improve the immune system. Laughter in all its forms has numerous health benefits, and I'm convinced it has spiritual benefits as well. Have you ever laughed so hard with others it felt like an act of worship? The joy that comes along with laughter is a gift from the Father. Laughter has a way of burying itself in our memories and uniting us with others. It can lighten a heavy heart. Laughter is a gift, and when used in the appropriate manner, one that glorifies the God who created it.

Song: *Joy* by Rend Collective

How's my heart today?

Attitude of gratitude:

Keep going: Laughter is an interesting form of non-verbal communication found throughout the Bible. It is a unique form of communication with a myriad of meanings depending on the situation. We see laughter taking place in what appears to be bitterness and unbelief (Genesis 18:13), as a form of righteousness (Psalm 52:6-7) and joy (Psalm 126:2). God also laughs (Psalm 37:12-13). When God laughs, it changes things. It intercedes for us. It provides more than just joy; it provides safety as He laughs in the face of the enemy. Have you ever considered God's laughter to be protection and victory over you?

DAY SEVEN

My third son makes questionable life decisions. Recently, he jumped off the bus and immediately I knew something was amiss.

"What's wrong?" I asked him casually, bracing myself for the worst.

His two older brothers chimed in for him. "He bought his lunch today! He's not supposed to do that!"

I put my arm around my youngest son and asked him to tell me the story. He looked up at me, tears in his eyes, and began to explain. "Well," he said, "I forgot my lunch in the classroom today. And I was starving. I wasn't sure what to do and I needed to eat, so I got in line and got some lunch."

"That's okay! I never want you to go hungry. Would the teachers at lunch not allow you to go back and grab your lunch?" I asked.

His eyes darted around as we started to walk home from the bus stop. He began looking for a new story line.

"Actually, it was Go Texan Day at school, and they were serving barbeque and I really wanted some," he said.

"Okay..." I trailed off, wondering why he was changing his story. "If you wanted to buy lunch today, you just had to ask. Remember what we talk about all the time, though, not giving the full truth is bound to get you in trouble."

When we got in the house, he threw his backpack on the ground and began to empty its contents. He pulled out his lunchbox and placed it on the counter. I unzipped it to find it empty. The saga of the lunch continued.

"Son, your lunch is empty. I'm wildly confused now. You said first you forgot your lunch. Then you said you just wanted to buy lunch. Now I'm seeing an empty lunch. Can you explain all of this to me?"

On cue, he began to cry, hoping he would score some sympathy points.

"Ok, Mom. This is the *real* story: I ate my lunch **and** I bought lunch," he said with manufactured tears streaming his flushed cheeks.

One of my other sons, as if this story of twists and turns needed any more plot points, casually added, "Mom, they didn't serve barbeque in the cafeteria for lunch today. It was pizza."

Exasperated, confused, and exhausted from the lunch saga, I questioned my son...again.

"Dude, I'm going to owe about $8 for your little joyride in the cafeteria today because you had no money on your account. Let's have the full story, please," I said.

My son started again, "Ok, this is the real *real* story: The teachers were having barbeque today and that sounded good to me. I wanted to try buying my lunch and pizza was what they served, so I bought it. Pizza sounded good too. And then I ate my entire lunch you packed for me. I'm growing and I need a lot of food."

Set free by the truth, he walked off, tear-free and with a clean conscious, to resume his normal activities. I continued to stand glued to my spot in the kitchen, attempting to process the story and connect the dots. Barbeque. Pizza. Forgotten lunch yet eaten lunch. A seven-year-old's story was too much for me to rationally understand. And in the end, it cost me $8.

For a long time, I thought reading God's Word would be a weaving, tangled story, much like my son's, that would require seminary in order to understand. I now know Scripture doesn't require formal education in order to be understood; it requires a surrendered heart and a willingness to hear from God. The Bible is not written for me to fit it comfortably into my circumstances. It is written to reveal the heart of God, and in turn, to transform me to look more like Him. God's holy and sacred Word is not intended to fit a mold of my making. I'm meant to be changed into looking more like Jesus through it. When I sit to spend time in the living Word of

God Himself, I know I'm reading a story that won't lead me astray. I will only find truth and life in the words that fill the pages. And for every season of life, for every new path God leads my family down, His Word remains the same.

> "In the beginning was the Word, and the Word was with God, and the Word was God" (John 1:1).

This powerful and gorgeous truth overwhelms me. The words I'm fortunate enough to read **are** my God. Today, and for days to come, let Scripture overwhelm you. Let it inspire you, transform you, embrace you and amaze you. Let it draw you to your knees and allow you to lift your praise. His Word, the simple yet complex story of His great love, won't cost you $8...it will cost you your life. And in return, you'll gain a life more beautiful than you ever imagined.

> "I have been crucified with Christ. It is no longer I who live, but Christ who lives in me" (Galatians 2:20).

Song: *How Great Thou Art* by Aaron Ivey

How's my heart today?

Attitude of gratitude:

Keep going: The Gospels of Matthew, Mark and Luke are referred to as synoptic because they recount similar stories. The Gospel of John contrasts the first three and begins with a different depiction of Jesus. Like Genesis, it starts, "In the beginning." Read John 1:1-18 in light of what you already know about Jesus. Find something in those first 18 verses that stands out in a way that never did before.

DAY EIGHT

It was a good thing I was at the cardiologist, because my heart beat at such a frantic pace I thought it may pop right out of my chest. And if it was going to do that, I was glad I was in the presence of doctors who specialize in fixing that kind of thing.

I was ushered back to a room by a kind nurse named Marci. I sat on the loud and crinkly white paper atop the exam table. I fought back tears, but I didn't know where they came from. Marci checked my vitals, input them into the system, and beckoned the doctor. He walked in, shook my hand, and asked me to move from the sterile table high above the floor to the seat next to him. Here, we could talk about all the matters of my heart.

I walked him through the pains that shot down my left arm, the tightness in my chest I had been feeling, and the dizzy spells. We ruled out my diet, my caffeine intake and a lack of exercise as roots to the problem. Another nurse tapped the door and rolled in a cart. I lifted my shirt and she placed stickers across my chest and shoulders. She then hooked the lines of the EKG machine to my stickers, asked me to be very still, and let the machine do the work. Within a matter of seconds, the patterns of my heart showed up on her screen.

The doctor evaluated the results and assured me the matter of my heart was actually no matter of the heart at all. My heart was healthy, for now, but my lifestyle wasn't. Due to my anxiety and stress levels, my body was imitating some of the signs of heart disease. And while it wasn't adversely wearing away at my organ now, eventually it would. I would need a lifestyle change.

What do we do in those moments? What do we do when we realize our condition doesn't have a quick fix? How do we rest, find calm, and quiet our drive to "do all the things" so we can get our hearts back to a place where they can do the job they were assigned to do?

My inability to rest was causing one of my major organs to mimic the signs of heart disease. My prescription was to find a way to minimize stress. It isn't easy to prune away at things in our lives causing us the heart conditions in the first place. It's easier to just keep saying yes when people ask us to volunteer more, give more, strive more, and do more. It's easier to fill our schedules and empty our tanks. But we simply cannot find rest for our souls when our souls cannot find time to be alone with the Father. The lists are daunting. The idea of letting others down is debilitating. But we have to start somewhere, and that somewhere is in making it a priority to connect with the Father. Time with Jesus is sacred and cannot be the first thing to come off a list because others would like to be added on.

God knew before the dawn of time we would run ourselves ragged. And yet, He does not give up on pursuing us and teaching us about His rest. He continues to call, and His call is out of love. Wondering where to start to lighten your load and fix that aching deep in the chambers of your heart? Come to Him. Come.

"Come to me, all who labor and are heavy laden, and I will give you rest" (Matthew 11:28).

Song: *Threads* by David Leonard

How's my heart today?

Attitude of gratitude:

Keep going: I don't always listen to God the first time. In fact, I don't always listen the second (or third) time, either. Sometimes I get so stubborn I think my way of living will be better because it's hard for my mind to fathom how such a big God could care about my day-to-day dwelling. This can lead to hard seasons, such as stress that mimics heart disease, in order to get me to full stop and surrender everything to Jesus. One of my favorite books of the Bible is Jonah. Read this book in its entirety and watch what happens when Jonah disagrees with God's call (multiple times) and contrast this with how God responds. We may be met with difficult circumstances at times because our own sinful nature has driven us there. God wants our whole hearts, and He will do anything to get them. What can you surrender to God today?

DAY NINE

I'm convinced love presents itself in the form of a homemade chicken pot pie. Sitting on the countertop to greet me when I returned home from a discouraging doctor's appointment, the smell radiated through the house and embraced me like a warm blanket. The kids ran frantically around the kitchen island, eagerly awaiting the go-ahead to dig in. I scooped it onto plates along with a side of fresh fruit. We sat around the table, and we devoured the meal as if it were the first we had in weeks. The crust crumbled delicately as our forks pushed through it to the perfectly gooey center, spilling out plump pieces of chicken and vegetables. Little was said between the forkfuls that met our mouths, but the feeling was mutual; this was exactly what we all needed.

I fought against this gift. Hard. I fought this life-giving opportunity for someone to take time and bless us with food. As I ate, the hardness of my heart crumbled like the crust of the chicken pot pie. Love and healing happened there. It happened in the breaking of buttery crusts, in the crunching of ripe berries, and in the moist bites of chocolate chip bread for dessert. This receiving of gifts from others was where healing and fixing and mending of messy and broken hearts were slowly, intricately sewn back together. And I almost missed it, all because I struggled to ask for help.

We're able to see the Father better when we allow others to serve us. Jesus told His disciples He did not embody human flesh so He could be served, but instead so He could serve (Mark 10:45). We were put here to serve, but there will be times, no doubt, when we will be on the receiving end of another's service. And when we deny others an opportunity to serve us, we deny them an opportunity to look like Jesus.

It isn't always easy to be served. The world calls us to be independent go-getters who rely on the hustle of our own efforts. But the truth is, we are designed to need and rely on others at times. We are created to serve others, and in turn, allow others to serve us. What if it's right there in the bursting open of the doors to the hard places of our own lives that we are truly able to help heal others too? What if that's where their healing comes - from serving in the way they were designed? From the showing of love and grace and mercy to those around them that need help because the God of the universe knit it into the fiber of their being? Being weak allows others a chance to be strong. And it allows God a chance to shine.

Don't miss an opportunity to allow someone to serve you simply because the world wants to paint the picture that accepting help makes you weak. You are no less of a person for surrendering to the authentic service of others. You may just find in allowing others to use their giftings to serve you, God will raise up a desire in your heart to serve others more fervently than before.

Song: *The Table* by Chris Tomlin

How's my heart today?

Attitude of gratitude:

Keep going: John 13:12-17 recounts when Jesus washed His disciples' feet. Read this in contrast to Luke 7:36-50 where a woman washes Jesus' feet with her tears. Her act of service saved her life. How do these two areas of Scripture help form your understanding of both serving and being served?

DAY TEN

I sat across from an old friend from high school in a dimly lit, trendy restaurant in downtown Houston. We occupied the end of the table, my husband sat next to me and a slew of friends filled the remainder of the seats. Scattered across each open space of table were delectable appetizers in celebration of my husband's birthday. I reached forward and prodded a piece of apple with my fondue stick, feeling as if this macaroni-and-cheese mom was completely out of her element. But there I sat, with an old friend, as we discussed our great passion for books and writing.

"I can write, but I don't have a story to tell," he said discouraged, each day the dream of writing his own books feeling farther from his grasp.

I looked up at him, instantly flooded with memories of sitting next to him in high school English, wishing for just an ounce of his writing talent. He now works as a successful CPA who travels the world crunching big numbers for big companies. Lodged deep within his heart, though, lies dormant a dream to write.

"I just don't have a story," he repeated.

I'm not sure in that moment I offered the right words. I may even have agreed with him because I, too, have fallen victim to believing my own gift is only useful if I have some fantastic and magnificent story to tell. But the truth is, we all have a story to tell, and we all have different means of telling it.

The over-saturated digital world can make anyone feel like the only way to successfully use one's gift is to use it in a way that instantly impacts large numbers of people. Looking for fame, influence, the perfect story or the perfect moment of inspiration, we may push our giftings aside if those moments and platforms don't manifest.

I can't do **the thing** until I have a **big thing** to do.

I've repeated those words in my own head millions of times.

What I've come to understand is those words are a lie of the enemy, a tactic slyly utilized by the one who wants to stifle our curiosity, creativity and passion. Don't believe that lie. Embrace your gift - whatever God has given you - and use it right now. The next moment before you is the most important moment because it's now. It's a moment to step further in faith, to look more like Jesus, to be salt and light in a world shrouded by darkness and parched for taste. We don't need the big moments to make a difference. We need the courage to look like Jesus in the moments we're in right now.

All of us have a story to tell and that is the heart of what we do. Jesus has taken something old and dirty and unqualified and made it new, clean and called. That is your story. Your story is your ministry, and your ministry doesn't need a brand because it is already branded by and for Christ.

Tell your story in the way you parent. Tell your story in the way you lead. Tell your story in the way you love a broken world. Tell your story in the way you live. Use the gifts God gives you to tell the world the greatest story of all - God's love story for all of us.

Song: *The Cause of Christ* by Kari Jobe

How's my heart today?

Attitude of gratitude:

Keep going: Open your Bible to 2 Corinthians 5:17-21. Read those verses slowly a few times. The story God has given to you is a gift, and it is an eternal one. How will you share it today?

DAY ELEVEN

I got the email as I was cleaning out junk drawers. I was trying to prepare; if I got the job, we'd have to make a quick move to Dallas, and I wanted to be ready. My phone blinked. I looked over at the notification, stopped what I was doing, and pulled up the email.

It was a generic response. "Thank you so much for your interest.... we are currently considering other applicants for this position."

I dropped my phone to the counter and stared blankly ahead. As the news sank in that all those hours I spent interviewing and compiling marketing assignments for the job resulted in another closed door, I began to cry. I wanted this job. I traveled to interview for this job. I was willing to uproot my family for this job. And after weeks of waiting, I didn't get the job. *Why, God, is my inbox full of rejections? Why have we received nothing but rejections for the last two years? What is wrong with me? Why do I keep failing?*

God was quick to reply to my aching heart. A closed door is not failure. A closed door can be a blessing. It can even be a cause for celebration.

I carried His reply with me for the rest of the day, dwelling on the gentle sound of His voice as I worked to receive those words. At dinner, as we went around the table sharing our high and low points of the day, I let my family in on the news.

"I didn't get the job, but hurry and eat your dinner," I told my kids as I shoveled food in my mouth. "You can stay up past your bedtime tonight. We are going out for dessert!"

Each of them cast me a confused glance.

"Why are we going out for dessert, Mom? Aren't you sad you didn't get the job?" my son asked.

"I am sad, but tonight we're going to celebrate rejection. Tonight, we're going to celebrate closed doors, because when God closes a door, it means there's something even better waiting just for us. God instructs us to look different from the world. If the world wants us to feel failure and defeat when a door closes, then we will choose to look like God and celebrate in faith and hope for what's to come," I said.

The world wants us to feel beat up, like a failure, miserable and downtrodden when a door closes.

But God.

"Do not be conformed to this world, but be transformed by the renewal of your mind, that by testing you may discern what is the will of God, what is good and acceptable and perfect" (Romans 12:2). God swoops in and tells us that, yes, sometimes He closes doors because there's something better behind a different door. And, yes, God can use the sting of defeat to teach us and transform us to look more like Him. I wanted to celebrate **that**. I wanted to celebrate that throughout this journey my family learned to pray together, to trust God's provisions when the bank account told us otherwise, and that looking and loving more like Jesus meant learning how to deal with defeat like He would.

That night, we looked drastically different from a family in the wake of defeat. Our lips were lined with chocolate ice cream and we laughed. The rejection still stung but stepping out in celebration of believing God was a God of His promises was salve for my weary soul. If the world wanted me defeated and broken by an email, then I was going to give the world a believer in Jesus who got ice cream instead.

There is something bigger. Something better. Something that our God is fashioning just for us. The enemy, instead of me, can taste the bitter sting of defeat in the midst of our celebration because with God on my side, there is no mountain that cannot be moved. It is not about celebrating the closed door; it is about celebrating our God who is bigger than all the closed doors we'll encounter. And when we change our perspective, we change how we live.

Sister, get an ice cream to celebrate today. Celebrate what God is doing and what He will do in your life. Celebrate that we as believers are called to look different from the world around us and that means stepping into our suffering and hurt and trusting our God is victorious over it all. And when we look more like Jesus and less like the world, we become a light so bright no closed door can ever put us out. He has conquered the grave and He will overcome whatever obstacles we face. And one day, when we live in perfect harmony with our loving Father in heaven, perhaps we'll eat chocolate ice cream together, and the only tears will be those of immense joy.

Song: *Share This Burden* by David Leonard

How's my heart today?

Attitude of gratitude:

Keep going: Read 1 Thessalonians Chapter 1. Paul uses the word "elect" or "chosen" in the same way other New Testament writers, like Peter, do - as a blessing. We are God's chosen children, set apart to do His work. Paul wrote to the church in Thessalonica because not only were they set apart, but they were doing it well. They were setting an example. Verse 7 uses the word "example" and in the Greek this word is tupos, which means "a stamp or scar" or "of a figure or image."[1] To be an example for Christ is to leave a mark on others in such a way that it changes them. Leave your mark on someone today.

---

[1] Joseph Thayer, "tupos," in *Thayer's Greek-English Lexicon of the New Testament*, rev. and ed. C.G. Wilke (Harper & Brothers, 2010), 632.

DAY TWELVE

My son's kindergarten teacher sent the following email to parents of her students:

"Hi All-

As I was working with a group today, some students decided to give themselves a haircut rather than doing the read, write, build sight word work. Some [haircuts are] more noticeable than others. We review scissor rules daily, but could you please have a conversation with your child that we should only cut paper? Thanks for your help in this matter."

As if a kindergarten teacher doesn't have it hard enough, this poor woman had to deal with a few kids thinking that day was a good one to explore techniques in hair cutting. *This poor woman will need a full day at the spa by the end of this week*, I thought to myself. Having already had this teacher two previous years, I knew she was a steady hand and not easily rattled. It wasn't often we received emails from her about kids not being on task.

I closed my laptop and went about my day, checking things off my to-do list without another thought about the email. In fact, I completely forgot about it until one of my sons jumped off the bus with a new haircut. Chunks of his beautiful blonde hair were missing from the front and sides. He smiled a big, goofy smile and walked right past me, as if business was as usual. And there I stood, my jaw hitting concrete, on that same spot where he told me the adventurous tale about how he wanted barbeque for lunch but ended up with pizza. I may start going to the bus stop in bare feet because that spot must be holy ground. It *must* be, because that's the spot where I keep receiving news that pushes all my mom buttons, and yet, by the power of God Himself, I don't lose it. It's holy ground, I tell you.

When I made it back into the house, I called the scissor perpetrator into the bathroom and further surveyed the damage. I could tell he went about the task of cutting his hair with the same precision and focus he was supposed to have given his classwork - hardly any area was left untouched. His hair stood up in some places, was cut into jagged edges in others, and overall just looked like he belonged in the clan of Herdmans. Remember the Herdmans, those six rowdy, always disheveled kids from *The Best Christmas Pageant Ever*? My kid looked like he belonged in a rag-tag group of hooligans who garnered little parental guidance.

"How did this happen?" I asked.

"I got bored," he responded.

"Did other kids do this too? Your teacher said in an email it was a group of students," I said.

"Yeah, my friend saw me do it and then thought it looked cool, so he did it too," he said proudly, as if he had accomplished a shining moment of leadership.

I dismissed him from the bathroom through clenched teeth and pulled out my computer to send an apology email to his teacher. I never thought I'd have to type the words, "I'm so sorry my child cut his hair in your class" once we hit elementary school, but as is typical with parenting, never say never.

A few days later, we buzzed the self-inflicted haircut down to its tiny hair nubs.

That third kid of mine makes some questionable choices. He knew better, but he did it anyway because the opportunity arose, and it seemed prime for the taking.

As frustrated as I get with some of his choices, I'm a lot like him. If we want to get really honest, we all are.

I make questionable choices when I'm scared or stressed. I cling to things of this world like financial security over Scripture; I yell when I should instead be on my knees. And I even try to force God's hand to move faster, turning the tides in my favor as to what is pleasing to me in that particular moment. In the brood of God's children, sometimes I'm the one with the scissors cutting my own hair.

And yet, even as I continue to chop away at things in my life, thinking I'm making them look or feel better, God doesn't push me away. He doesn't storm off in anger or keep tally. Instead, He's full of patience and steadfast love, never leaving or forsaking me. He guides me back to His heart where I can put the scissors down, rest in Him, and be restored.

Romans 8:31-32 says, "What then shall we say to these things? If God is for us, who can be against us? He who did not spare his own Son but gave him up for us all, how will he not also with him graciously give us all things?"

When I start to spiral, God doesn't leave me. He loves me. And this love is so big and so incredible it provides everything we would ever need. It's a sacrificial love, one where God willingly allowed His perfect Son to hang on a cross for all His rowdy kids who would walk through life trying to cut their own hair. Remember that today, dear sisters, as you face a day of choices. Some days you'll reach for the scissors, and some days you'll reach for Scripture. But His grace covers all, and each day He's making us look more like Him - messy haircuts and all.

Song: *Alive* by Hillsong Young & Free

How's my heart today?

Attitude of gratitude:

Keep going: Turn to Hebrews Chapter 1 in your Bible and read it in its entirety. Note in verse three it says "he sat down." A priest does not sit until the work is done. Jesus is sitting at the right hand of the Father. The work is done. It was finished when He took your place on the bloody cross. We deserved those splintered pieces of wood and flesh-driving nails, but He took it. In what ways do you need to surrender your scissors today? (If you're willing to go even further, the full depth and beauty of Hebrews is best understood when studied with Numbers.)

DAY THIRTEEN

I returned home from the emergency room in the crisp night air. I was used to emergency room visits with my children, but it wasn't often I succumbed to the necessity to go myself. When the blazing, searing rash brought about by shingles burst forth on my scalp and into my right eye, I went. The diagnosis was disheartening and the prescription for healing even more so: I would have to rest.

I dismissed the doctor's orders to go straight to bed when I got home and instead emailed my boss. I wrote four apologetic paragraphs. I explained my diagnosis on a Thursday meant I would need only one day off; I would be back to work Monday. Never mind the immense stress I carried and needed to unload in order to heal, I was too worried about looking weak to my boss and co-workers.

The enemy, in a state of complete glory, took my diagnosis and made me feel inadequate. Fragile. Ashamed. Not worthy. And my overly determined heart wasn't aware I was pushing too hard, too fast, and without enough rest. I was missing my calling by a million miles and I was showing my kids a version of the gospel that was a farce. I wasn't living out that Jesus' sacrifice and grace were enough; I was worried about making myself enough. The enemy didn't want me to feel weak so God could be my strength. The enemy wanted me lonely and busy and tired and stubborn. He wanted my well to dry out and my dehydrated soul to seek refreshment in the things of this world.

The stress and anxiety I carried for so long slowly transferred to my children. I noticed it in the way they did homework and prepared for tests. I noticed it in the way they modeled my lifestyle of striving. My life didn't look like a gospel of grace, it looked like exhaustion. As a model for Christ to my children, something had to change. Hustle, striving and proving had to go.

The world doesn't need my hustle for it to still spin, and the Kingdom certainly doesn't need my hustle in order to grow. It needs my heart. My *surrendered* heart.

Jesus didn't hustle. Jesus fed 5000 with the miracle of multiplying five loaves of bread and two fish. And when He was finished, "he went up on the mountain to pray" (Mark 6:46). Alone. Jesus performed a miracle and then stole away to rest. Scripture does not reference Jesus living His life in hurried moments, cutting corners to increase productivity. He worked and rested, never apologizing for the time He took to be with His Father. The rhythm of Jesus' life is one to be modeled; often I want to model Him as teacher, but I squirm when urged to model His suffering and rest. The world values hustle and puts little emphasis on rest. But Scripture repeatedly calls us to a different rhythm of living.

Jesus models that rest is not optional; it is an indispensable requirement for believers. Rest draws us closer to God, it quiets the raging world around us, and it allows our bodies to function at a greater capacity - spiritually, emotionally, mentally and physically. God can do more in a day with our surrendered hearts than we could do in a lifetime of hustle.

May this verse be our living water as we work to find our place of stillness and rest with the Lord:

> "Come to me, all who labor and are heavy laden, and I will give you rest. Take my yoke upon you, and learn from me, for I am gentle and lowly of heart, and you will find rest for your souls. For my yoke is easy, and my burden is light" (Matthew 11:28-30).

Song: *Be Still My Soul (In You I Rest)* by Kari Jobe

How's my heart today?

Attitude of gratitude:

Keep going: Read Matthew 14:13-24. The first time Jesus retreats in this passage is in verse 13 in grief over the death of John the Baptist. Crowds followed Him. Everywhere Jesus went there were hungry to be fed, sick to be healed, challengers who needed answers. The work never ceased, but Jesus had moments where He ceased to work because of the value placed on rest. The first time rest is recorded in the Bible is in Genesis when God rested on the seventh day. If the rhythm of a triune God is to rest **even when there is still work left to complete**, then we should adapt that rhythm too. How can you implement rest into daily living?

DAY FOURTEEN

One of my favorite stories happens after the resurrection of Jesus. John records it in John 21:1-14.

Simon Peter decided to go fishing one night on the Sea of Tiberias. A handful of other disciples joined him. They cast their nets time and time again yet caught nothing. These fishers of men under the direction of Jesus were now reverting back to their original trade, only to be met with empty nets. As the sun summoned the start of a new day, Jesus stood on the shore. Jesus called out to them, "Children, do you have any fish?" They called back with a solemn, "No." Jesus told them to cast their net on the right side of the boat. Sure enough, the net became so full of fish they couldn't even pull it back into the boat. John recognized it was the Lord Jesus on the bank, and Simon Peter, completely overcome with emotion, jumped ship and swam to shore. The others stayed in the boat and hauled in their enormous catch.

Jesus was beside a charcoal fire cooking fish waiting for the men. A loaf of bread awaited the hungry fishermen too. John records the men caught 153 fish and, at the request of their Savior, they brought a few of those fish to the well-tended fire. And there, at the break of day, Jesus made his friends breakfast.

This is one of my favorite stories for a multitude of reasons. One may be that I have a special place in my heart for three of the key components of the story: sunrises, beaches and breakfast. I also can't help but let my mind wander to recreate that scene in my head when Simon Peter jumps ship after realizing the resurrected Jesus is on the shore. I wonder if Jesus chuckled to Himself when Simon Peter, full of more joy than he could contain in his human body, jumped out of the boat. Simon Peter didn't care about the 153 fish that needed hauling in, and he didn't even consider if his fellow fishermen could handle the load. He just jumped ship. I imagine the other men in the boat snickered a bit too…until they realized they were one able-bodied man short of hauling in a big catch.

And then I wonder, am I like Peter? When I see Jesus at work, calling out to me, do I jump out of the boat and go to Him? Or do I sit back and make sure everything is in place before I'm obedient? I think there are days when I want to be like Peter; I want to be so obedient I jump ship without thinking. I want to swim the lengths necessary without even questioning how far Jesus is asking me to go. I just go.

I'm deeply moved that Jesus' appearance to His disciples was in the posture of service. His body broken on the cross, scars still intact, the Savior of the world continued to serve those around Him.

And He did so with a hearty breakfast by the sea. As the gentle waves lapped the shoreline, Jesus sat huddled with His disciples and He fed them. There was bread. There were fish. But I have a feeling the disciples were fed in a way no earthly food could satisfy.

Song: *The Road, The Rocks, and The Weeds* by John Mark McMillan

How's my heart today?

Attitude of gratitude:

Keep going: Remember Peter's denial? Peter sure did. The scene set in John 21:1-14 sets up a gorgeous moment for Jesus and Peter that follows that denial. Read verses 15-25 remembering this was in the wake of both Peter's denial and Jesus' miraculous resurrection. The same Jesus that forgave and commissioned Peter on the beach is the same Jesus who forgives and commissions you right where you are. What does Jesus need you to do today with your gifts?

DAY FIFTEEN

I pray my children will grow up to be warriors for Christ.

I chose the word warriors for multiple reasons. Warriors instead of worriers; warriors who fight to take the gospel to the world around them; warriors who fight for justice; and warriors who fight for their personal walk with God their entire lives, never allowing themselves to become complacent in the Good News.

While I pray this over my children daily, I try not to over-spiritualize things at home. I want our home to be an open place for them to worship, read Scripture, pray and ask questions. I don't ever want to become so rigid in my own perception of each of their walks with Christ that I make it legalistic and difficult for them. Not everything we talk about has to circle back to a Bible lesson, but when I mess up, the best way for them to understand Christ-like forgiveness is for me to fess up. Fess up when you mess up – the beautiful collision of grace and mercy, and a Fraser family motto.

First grade homework sometimes makes me white-knuckled, fist-clinched frustrated. Whether it's because my son doesn't want to do his homework or there's a problem I don't understand, homework seems to be a battle in our house. And one Tuesday afternoon, I let the homework win. I raised my voice. I got angry. I raised my voice some more and slammed a pencil on the table. My raised voice woke a child from his nap. For a few minutes of an otherwise good day, homework got the best of me. And I was ashamed.

I was painstakingly aware my behavior was unnecessary and an overreaction. I knew I messed up, and the only way out of the situation was to ask my son (and everyone in the house witnessing me losing my mind over a math problem) for forgiveness. Fess up when you mess up.

But it was the morning after the incident that changed everything. I sat at our kitchen table doing my morning Bible study and the child who was abruptly awoken from his nap due to my yelling locked eyes on me. I put my pen down and looked at him. A drop of his cereal milk rested on his chin.

"Mommy, you look like God." His words hung in the air. "Except when you yelled yesterday."

I wasn't sure how to respond. I stuttered out questions, "I? Me? Look like who? When?"

He repeated his words.

"You look like God."

I stared at him and he returned to eating his cereal, as if the most powerful words had not just left his lips.

I have never been likened to God before. Sure, I understand I'm made in His image, but I have never looked in the mirror and felt I was looking at God Himself. Instead, I see the millions of ways I fall short and the sin caked on in layers that at times hardens my heart. I see someone who yells over homework and fails to offer grace in situations when it's desperately needed. I see someone forgiven but still so flawed. I see someone who loves Jesus but definitely isn't a textbook model of Him. I've said it many times before and I'll say it again: I'm broken and messy and most days I think I'm getting this mom thing all wrong.

But perhaps I need a new lens. Perhaps I need to see myself the way God sees me, as a child of God, wonderfully made in His image, His delight and loved by Him first.

1 John 4:12 says, "No one has ever seen God; if we love one another, God abides in us and His love is perfected in us."

Can you imagine if we woke up every day and looked in the mirror and saw ourselves shrouded in grace? If we saw ourselves through the lens of the sacrificial love of Jesus so then we could see glimpses of God in us and in others? Can you imagine if we granted ourselves and others the same grace our Savior gifts us daily?

It could change the world.

Let's go change the world.

Song: *We Could Change the World* by Matt Redman

How's my heart today:

Attitude of gratitude:

Keep going: Turn to Acts 22. Read verses 1 - 21. Paul testified on his own behalf after his arrest. Notice when Paul gives his defense he starts with where he was (a Pharisee who persecuted Christians) and then talks about where he is now that he follows Jesus. Despite the sin flooding his past, Paul knows the calling Jesus has given him. He doesn't shy away from it simply because the man he sees in the mirror once persecuted the ones he is now called to minister to. Jesus calls the unworthy and broken to do His mighty work, and Paul now sees his life through that lens. What do you see when you look in the mirror? How is that perception changed when you look through the lens of Jesus' sacrificial and grace-filled love?

DAY SIXTEEN

My memory is failing me lately. After loading the washing machine, I couldn't remember if I put in the laundry detergent pod. My body halfway in the giant machine, I dug through smelly, dirty clothes to see if I could find the cleaning agent. My initial search yielded no results, so I removed all of the clothes, shook them out, and searched the washer again. Sure enough, tucked in the corner of the machine, the detergent pod sat completely untouched. I reloaded the laundry in a fit of irritation and tried to remind myself to be more aware the next time around.

Forty minutes later, I was doing the same thing again.

And then I remembered I could have just thrown another pod in and it wouldn't have done any harm.

My memory is failing me. I can't remember when my children last took a bath, if the dishes in the dishwasher are clean or dirty, or where I placed the latest progress report that needs to be signed and returned. Where has my memory, once sharp, gone? I fear it will only get worse from here, though.

I've had to ask myself a tough question regarding my memory lately. Do I remember I'm loved by God? If I'm being honest, there are days when I don't remember I'm loved by the One who authored life itself. I often have to dig through the lies of my mind (placed there by the enemy himself) to find the cleaning agent that washes me pure. Even though I'm surrounded by the love letters of God, I'm quick to forget I am His beloved.

My parents said it first to me. I said it first to my children. And one day down the road, my children will hold their new babies in their arms and say it first too. Three words that have forever changed the course of history: I love you.

Let's rewind back to the beginning of time when "God created the heavens and the earth. The earth was without form and void, and darkness was over the face of the deep. And the Spirit of God was hovering over the face of the waters" (Genesis 1:1-2). Now flash-forward to Jesus's life and then brutal death on the cross. Three days later, the tomb was empty. Death was overcome. And why? Why the pain and heartache of the cross and the joy and hope of the empty tomb? Why does our story begin just as much on that first day of creation as it does the day death was defeated?

"For God so loved the world, that he gave his only Son" (John 3:16).

It was all for love, and that love was all for us. Our lungs are full of breath because of His love. Jesus died on the cross because of His love. God muttered those words over His beloved creation first.

What if we responded to Him not with an "I love you" only, but with an additional word in the phrase, I love you **too**? How could we forget the expanse of His great love if we learn to respond to Him with one additional word reminding us His love came first, not second?

We aren't worthy of a love like that. We fall so short it took the sacrifice of God's only Son to redeem us. We aren't the creators or the owners or the parents. We are the children first held. The children first loved.

For that, Father, we humbly and adoringly reply, "We love you too."

Song: *Your Glory/Nothing But The Blood* by All Sons & Daughters

How's my heart today?

Attitude of gratitude:

Keep going: David beautifully illustrates God's love in Psalm 103. Underline each of the attributes of God and remember God is exactly who He says He is. He will never fail you. He will never leave you. And you will never be loved by anyone more than God loves you.

DAY SEVENTEEN

Jesus can use pizza to spread His message of love.

Spring evenings in Texas, when the air is warm, the sun is bright and the humidity is low, are like a tangible piece of heaven on earth. The neighborhood kids, enjoying the longer stretch of sunlight, started playing intense wiffle ball games in front of my house. They divided into equal teams, stood in line to take a whack at the small white ball, and everyone cheered when it soared overhead. Never mind running the bases, this game was all about the excitement of hitting the ball. Junior high kids even stopped for a few swings at home plate before heading home for dinner. Faces were red and smiles were wide, but when the dinner bell rang and everyone had to return home, a bit of disappointment lingered in the air.

One Friday I decided the fun wouldn't stop at dinner time. I invited all 14 kids outside of my home to stay on the driveway for cheese pizza. Our neighborhood is made up of people from all different countries, backgrounds and religions. Pizza would be our unifier that day.

When the delivery man arrived with a front seat full of piping hot cheese pizzas, the kids circled on the driveway. The night before I chalked "Smile! Jesus loves you!" across the spot where they all stood. And as if that wasn't gorgeous enough, the moms of the kids started pouring onto my driveway. We had a Muslim family from Pakistan, a woman from Egypt who told me once at the bus stop she wasn't a believer, a Buddhist family, and a Hispanic woman with broken English. It was the most beautiful display of cultural diversity.

And there we were, neighbors congregated atop the words "Jesus loves you!" enjoying the ministry of cheese pizza.

The women communicated their gratitude for dinner through hugs and smiles. One of my neighbors, who I had yet to meet face-to-face, said she was nervous to meet people in America. It was hard to come from Pakistan, she said, and she prayed for neighbors who were safe and kind. What I thought would just be a fun treat for the neighborhood kids turned into an evening where I could serve and love my neighbors. This was so much more than pizza. This was an evening of living out the words of Jesus.

I may not have been able to share the full gospel with those women that night, but they stood on the words I most wanted them to remember: Jesus loves you. Each woman, delicately and beautifully created by God, stood atop words she may not fully understand and believe yet. But they were there, unwavering and true.

I was reminded of Paul's words, "I have become all things to all people, that by all means I might save some. I do it all for the sake of the gospel, that I may share with them in its blessings" (1 Corinthians 9:22-23). Sometimes we have to become the bearers of cheese pizza to bring the gospel and its message of love and hope. Jesus said to love your neighbors, and when He said it, He meant it.

Song: *Here As In Heaven* by Elevation Worship

How's my heart today?

Attitude of gratitude:

Keep going: The Pharisees were rigid followers of the law and sought to destroy Jesus by finding ways He contradicted the law. In Matthew 22:34-40, the Pharisees wanted to know which law was the "greatest." Read Jesus' response and then find a way today to love your neighbor.

DAY EIGHTEEN

My daughter climbed onto the couch and snuggled into my side. Her warmth comforted me and her gentle breaths, the rising and falling of her chest, eased my anxious soul. It had been one of those parenting weeks, where all the kids seemed to team up and decide how to best wreak havoc. I had been pulled in a thousand directions all at once.

My other daughter climbed up on the couch to join us, vigorously sucking her pointer finger.

"Mommy, my teachers say, 'Use kind words, keep your hands to yourself,'" my oldest daughter said. She smiled with the satisfaction of remembering the rules from preschool. I wrapped her in a hug, kissed the top of her head and told her I was proud of her for remembering such important things. I got up from the couch to grab a water, and not 30 seconds later I heard the high-pitched squeal of my youngest daughter.

I darted back to the couch to find the rule-reciter pinching her sister on the soft underside of the arm.

"No! Don't do that! You just told me the rules are to 'Use kind words and keep your hands to yourself' so why are you pinching your sister?" I reprimanded.

Her smile turned upwards with a sly curve and she released her sister's skin from within her pinched fingers. She then shrugged her shoulders at me and walked off to resume her morning activities.

Like I said, it's been quite the parenting week. Or month. Or year. To be honest, I can't quite remember. I just know my daughter knows the rules down pact but can't seem to translate them into a lifestyle, and that's about the norm around this house right now. I stopped drinking caffeine a while ago, but it may be a good time to fire up the coffee pot.

Or perhaps I could use a bit of humbling in this arena too. Some days I'm the one remembering the words of Jesus but forgetting to live them out. How easy is it for me to read "love your neighbor" but then forget how to walk outside the comfort of my home and do that? How easy is it for me to read about my identity in Christ but then be quick to feel forgotten and unheard? And how easy is it for me to succumb to the desires of my flesh when Scripture makes it clear I'm to rely solely on Jesus?

I know the things my Bible says but I'm not always great at living them out.

Luckily our God is a God of infinite chances. He has not put a limit on how many times we can fall short. This does not give us a free pass to live however we please; however, it does provide us with grace upon grace as we navigate living in a fallen world. He simply asks that we come to Him, ask His forgiveness, and surrender our hearts. Dying daily must become our new lifestyle. When we enter into intimate closeness with God, the world has a harder time diverting our attention. We're much more capable of loving our neighbors, resting, waiting on the Lord, and praising Him through all seasons when we are in close relationship with Him.

We're bound to make mistakes because we're bound in a time period after the fall. But God doesn't let our story stop there.

> "Therefore, since we have been justified by faith, we have peace with God through our Lord Jesus Christ. Through him we have also obtained access by faith into this grace in which we stand, and we rejoice in hope of the glory of God. Not only that, but we rejoice in our sufferings, knowing that suffering produces endurance, and endurance produces character, and character produces hope, and hope does not put us to shame, because God's love has been poured into our hearts through the Holy Spirit who has been given to us" (Romans 5:1-5).

For us, the story continues. We wait in hopeful expectation that this endurance, character and hope building life prepares us for the perfect one that is to come. Today, we may forget how to live out what has been placed before us, but one day, we'll live in perfect bodies, our hearts focused on perpetual worship to the Creator, unbound and unshackled by the forgetfulness we suffer now.

Song: *Turn Your Eyes Upon Jesus* by Lauren Daigle

How's my heart today?

Attitude of gratitude:

Keep going: Read Romans 5:6-11. The job to rescue your soul has been completed. No powers of hell or even death can claim you, because your Savior was the ransom for them all. Underline the words "justified by his blood" in verse 9. Jesus' blood made you righteous and granted you access to the inheritance of God. These are powerful words with deep, life-changing meaning. What verse most challenges how you live out God's promises daily?

DAY NINETEEN

Comfort kills obedience.

In the last year, I've recited this phrase over and over. For a while, I created a false inverse to the statement, thinking if comfort killed obedience then discomfort was a by-product of obedience. I was wrong, of course, because I don't serve a God who wants my unrestrained devotion to Him so I can live a life of mere discomfort. What I had forgotten, and soon learned, was comfort can be the most dangerous thing to obedience, and no amount of discomfort can take away from the utter freedom, peace and joy obedience ushers in.

There's never a convenient time to be tight on cash, but having your finances stretched to their limits around Christmas may be the hardest. I knew when my fifth child was born God was calling me to be home for a season of rest. And while this would be the first time we were a single income family, I also knew in the deepest parts of my heart God would provide. What I didn't know was how difficult it would be at times to look at the bottom line of the bank account and wonder how we would afford groceries, gas or electricity.

We didn't confide our financial struggles to many, least of all our parents. We had made it 10 years of marriage without needing financial assistance, and our pride built a barrier around our vulnerability. We were honest with our children, though, because Christmas that year looked drastically different than years' past. It was refreshing, however, to be so honest as a family and remember in gratitude all God had done.

Along with a close-knit group of prayer warriors, we doubled down on prayer as a family. We fasted. We begged God to bring my husband a new job that would provide financially so I could stay in my place of obedience at home raising five kids. Our pride eventually broke, and we invited our families into our intimate financial situation, knowing the more prayer storming the gates of heaven, the better.

But no job came. Instead, miracles poured in. Money was left on our doorstep in cards, or it would suddenly appear in our Venmo account in the weeks leading up to Christmas. Many of those miracle workers who gave us money, most of which had no idea we were financially strapped, are still anonymous. And we would have missed each miracle, delicately wrapped in sacrificial love, if we weren't obedient. We would have missed the humbling opportunity of being on the receiving end of gift giving, learning how to parcel each cent in the most God glorifying way. We would have missed the tears of joy and wonderment we shared as a family as we opened envelopes or realized we could buy a few gifts for each other. There are a million little ways God carried us, and continues to carry us, as we lean hard into obedience.

Does this kind of obedience look crazy to some people? Absolutely.

Through it all, though, we learned obedience to God is not just a pretty saying we put on the walls of our house. It's a lifestyle. It's a change of perspective and a change of heart. It's a posture of dependence, on one's knees, knowing things may get uncomfortable along the journey but God provides more love and grace than can be expected, and certainly more than is ever deserved.

I don't know a lot of things, but I do know my desire to be comfortable - financially, socially, physically - will kill my obedience to the Father if I let comfort become the louder voice in my ear, the stronger tug on my heart. May our ears, eyes and hearts always be turned to the Father, longing desperately to live only for His glory and within His divine will. And when we live in that obedience, wholly dependent on Him, may our lips mutter praise and thanksgiving as we traverse both the mountains and the valleys.

Song: *Steadfast* by Sandra McCracken

How's my heart today?

Attitude of gratitude:

Keep going: Ready to really dig into your Scripture? Let's do a character study of a man with obedience unlike anything I've seen before – Abram (at this point in the story, he has not yet been renamed "Abraham"). Turn to Genesis 12. The first recorded words from God to Abram were, "Go from your country and your kindred and your father's house to the land that I will show you" (12:1). To understand the magnitude of this call, we have to realize a person's country, kindred and father's house were some of the most important pieces of a person's identity back then. This weaving of country and family provided community and provision. God instructs Abram with a single, powerful verb, "Go." God asked him to leave everything he knew and then left the details out. Abram didn't know the endpoint; he just knew God would lead the way. This is a model of obedience that transforms the heart and builds God's kingdom in gigantic ways. Read all of Genesis 12 today. Would you drop everything of comfort if God asked? To see more of Abram's radical obedience, follow his faith journey through Genesis. Want even more? Trace how he is referenced in the New Testament too!

DAY TWENTY

I tell them to brush their teeth, they assure me they're doing it, and then I find them playing in the sink.

We go through this same routine every night.

Eventually, all my children brush their teeth. In their wake, the bathroom counter looks like a battleground of used toothpaste and spit, and the counter suffers a great casualty. The remnants of their efforts cake hard and blue upon the white porcelain background, and without fail it requires elbow grease to remove. I'll never understand how such a simple task can result in such a grotesque display.

After they have brushed their teeth, somehow, they still aren't in bed. Each child requires roughly 10 glasses of water to quench his or her thirst. At this point, I don't care if they are in actual pajamas, the clothes they wore to school that day, or a new outfit for tomorrow. It's time to go to bed.

We alternate each night who will say prayers. Despite the most difficult 20 minutes of my day prior to this point, this is my favorite part of the day.

One night my oldest son began to pray over his youngest sister.

"And God, please let her have no sin in her, just like Jesus. This world is already full of sin, and we already have caught it, but please let her have no sin in her heart," he prayed.

I opened my eyes and looked upon him as he continued to pray. *What a prayer*, I thought.

It astounds me how my children often pray big, bold prayers without hesitation. And while praying for his sister to live sin-free may be the boldest prayer I've heard to date, I'm thankful nonetheless that my son chose that as his prayer. He felt called at that moment to pray protection over her from the sin of which we are already ensnared.

My prayer life has endured many seasons, but I don't think my prayers have ever been as bold as my son's.

> "Do not be anxious about anything, but in everything by prayer and supplication with thanksgiving let your requests be made known to God" (Philippians 4:6).

This was not a request by Paul. This was a command. Walking with Jesus is not possible without a prayer life that is alive and thriving, and a prayer life that is alive is a prayer life that brings everything to the throne of grace. Every request. All of them. Hold nothing back, sisters. Even though He knows what is on your heart, He desires for you to pray it boldly again and again and again.

Pray prayers that will change the world. Pray prayers that will save lives. Pray prayers that will scare the enemy into hiding. But promise yourself one thing: You won't hold back, because a woman on her knees in prayer is a woman who will not bend or bow to the world around her.

Song: *How Great Is Your Love* by Phil Wickham

How's my heart today?

Attitude of gratitude:

Keep going: We can't talk about prayer without talking about the prayer Jesus modeled for His disciples. Matthew 6:5-15 records it. Read it again, slowly taking in each word. Now write The Lord's Prayer. This prayer is a bold prayer, despite it being short in length. The power of your prayers do not depend on the length. They depend on the posture of your heart. What is your bold prayer today? Write it down.

DAY TWENTY-ONE

There's an episode of *Seinfeld* that cracks my husband and me up every time. In the episode, George and Jerry share a hotel room - and a bed. The housekeeping lady asks the pair how she can prepare the bed for them; would they like the sheets tucked in around the corners or left untucked? They quickly realize one prefers tucked while the other untucked, which leads to an interesting night.

This is my husband and me every night. When we first saw the episode, we laughed so hard we almost cried. I'm a tucker. I like my sheets tucked in so tight I feel like I'm part of the bed when I go to sleep. But my husband loves the sheets untucked. When he climbs into bed, he pulls and yanks them all over the place, making sure there's never too much restraint on his over six-foot frame. It drives me nuts, but after almost 10 years of marriage, we've just learned to make it work. I keep the sheet tucked on my side and his side looks like it was ravaged by wild animals.

My reasoning for tucked sheets is absurd, and I'm about to let you in on my secret fear driving my need for tucked in sheets. My fear is this: if my feet are exposed from under the safety of the covers, they could potentially fall victim to being cut off by an intruder.

Remember, I told you this was an absurd fear.

The problem is, I know how absurd and irrational it is. I know it's absolutely bonkers. But I proceed to live as one who prefers her sheets tucked in, just in case someone was to break into my house with the sole intention of collecting feet from the ankles down. Roll your eyes or laugh; my husband has done plenty of the two over the years. While you're laughing, I'm at least comfortable knowing no feet burglar is claiming me as the next victim.

Fear has a sly way of creeping into areas of our lives that at first seem harmless and then become so detrimental we are paralyzed by them. The more I've thought about fear, the more I realize it's a breeding ground for other ailments that impede upon my daily, obedient, Christ-following living. Fear of not being able to plan and control the future breeds anxiety. Fear of not being liked breeds people-pleasing. The list goes on and on. I've sat paralyzed by the offspring of fear too many times to count, and I'm not proud to admit it. But there's something about fear the enemy absolutely loves, and that's making fear seem normal. The enemy is skilled at making the darkness accompanying fear seem almost like light, and I'm not quite sure how he does it.

But the Bible speaks to fear in multiple places.

"Say to those who have an anxious heart,
'Be strong; fear not!
Behold, your God
will come with vengeance,
with the recompense of God.
He will come and save you'" (Isaiah 35:4).

"Therefore do not be anxious about tomorrow, for tomorrow will be anxious for itself. Sufficient for the day is its own trouble" (Matthew 6:34).

"There is no fear in love, but perfect love casts out fear" (1 John 4:18).

"Oh, how abundant is your goodness,
which you have stored up for those who fear you
and worked for those who take refuge in you,
in the sight of the children of mankind!" (Psalm 31:19).

Scripture instructs us to have a healthy fear of God, but we were not created to live in fear of the imagined. We were created to live in the light of our Father. In the darkness of fear and the many shadows it casts, there lies the slow destruction of our own hearts. Oftentimes fear will drive me to places of complete exhaustion, lending me to either succumb to the fear all together and stay defeated, or I draw strength from the truth of God's Word and stand up to it.

There's something marvelous about the weapons we're given to fight fear – they are supernatural. These are not weapons that can be destroyed by the world, but weapons that come from God Himself. When we arm ourselves for battle against fear, the one leading the charge is God. Perfect love comes only from Him. He goes before us to cast out the evil that wants to shackle us.

The days will have trouble, sisters. They will bring struggle and heartache in the same way they will bring triumph and joy. But we need not fear, because the Creator, the Healer, the Giver of Life and the Father of eternity has gone before us to cast out the darkness that wants to claim our hearts.

Tonight, and every night, I can untuck the sheets in complete confidence fear doesn't get the last word in my heart. Victory in Jesus does.

Song: *No Longer Slaves* by Bethel Music

How's my heart today?

Attitude of gratitude:

Keep going: Did you know the most common command in the Bible is "fear not"? God knew we would be a people shackled by the enemy's tactic of fear, and He didn't leave us without direction on how to conquer it. In Judges 6:11-40 we are introduced to a man who allowed fear to cast in him doubt and anxiety. Read how Gideon responded to God over and over again in those verses, and then continue in Chapter 7 to see what happened when Gideon allowed the power of God to overcome him and his fears. What fears can you surrender at the cross today?

DAY TWENTY-TWO

Her name is tattooed on my ribs.

I will always remember the way the needle felt as it pricked across the delicate skin stretched across my ribcage. Slowly, and in permanence, the word "joie" was etched.

"Joie" was my grandmother's nickname in high school, given to a woman with the birth name JoAnne yet with the demeanor of God's joy wrapped in flesh. In French, "joie" means joy. When I discovered that, I knew this word would be tattooed across my ribs to serve as a beautiful reminder of her life lived boldly and bravely for the Lord, as well as a reminder that the lungs underneath that ribcage were capable of inhaling and exhaling pure joy, no matter the season. As much as I shouldn't need reminding of that, some days I do.

And now, there it is, just about the width of my pointer finger, "joie" expands and contracts with each of my breaths.

Joy is also the name of my fifth child. There was a long season of adjusting to the realization we would have another child because she wasn't planned. In that season, we struggled at times to have joy. My children, family and friends stepped in to help carry joy for us while we struggled to find it. Our daughter would come to bring light and laughter, to round us out and make us better, to throw the plans we had made aside and align our lives even more with the Lord. But in those first few months after finding out we were pregnant, joy was difficult to come by.

There was worry and anxiety, fear and frustration. And then there was release. It was as if all the enemy's tactics to stronghold us into denying the goodness of God's plan had worn out. In the release of our own worries about the future, God became our Rescuer. Day by day we were able to better see how He worked all of this for His Kingdom. Our plans were nothing in comparison to His.

There's so much joy in realizing obedience and complete dependence on God means releasing all the things we thought were holding us stable. There's so much joy in the freedom of Christ. There's so much joy in wrapping yourself in the tender promises of the Father.

How could we name our daughter anything but Joy when she helped us understand the word on such a deeper level?

There's joy planted within you, too, and it's longing to unveil itself in new, miraculous ways. Release your worries, fears, shame, and guilt, and let joy blossom and transform you.

> "Though you have not seen him, you love him. Though you do not now see him, you believe in him and rejoice with joy that is inexpressible and filled with glory" (1 Peter 1:8).

Song: *Joyful Joyful* by ACM Gospel Choir

How's my heart today?

Attitude of gratitude:

Keep going: Joy can live in the tension of the hard and the glorious. According to Lexicon Bible Dictionary, joy is "closely related to gladness and happiness, although *joy is more a state of being than an emotion; a result of choice*" (emphasis mine).[2] There is so much to be said about joy. Have you ever done a word study in Scripture? While this is a big undertaking, start small and commit to finding 3-5 verses throughout the Bible that talk about joy. You can use the concordance in the back of your Bible to help locate verses with the word joy. How do these verses change your perception of joy?

[2] John D. Barry, David Bomar, Derek R. Brown et. al., "Joy" in *Lexham Bible Dictionary,* ed. John D. Barry, (Washington: Lexham Press, 2016).

DAY TWENTY-THREE

My oldest son is the most timid of my kids. He calculates the risk associated with everything, and if there's even a slight chance he could get hurt, he opts out. The rest of his siblings, however, just go for it. On a rare, perfect Texas afternoon, my adventurous middle child whizzed around my oldest on his training-wheel-free bike, taunting him. For the first time, despite his fears, my oldest son looked at me with confidence and determination.

"I'm ready to take my training wheels off," he said.

I nodded my head in approval and ran for the garage. I retrieved the necessary tools, opened the door to the house, and yelled for my husband to come out and witness a milestone. I took the training wheels off and rolled the bike to my son.

"Okay, are you ready? Don't be scared. You can do this. Just remember to look up. Visualize yourself riding with no training wheels. You won't fall. I'm right here the whole time," I said.

His unsure expression told me any confidence he started with was now gone.

"I'm going to fall," he said. "I know it."

"No, you won't. I'm right here with you."

We went back and forth for a few minutes until I finally convinced him to get on the bike. I gave him instructions to pedal as I held the back of his seat. I ran alongside him, smiling from ear to ear.

"I'm right here! You're doing it!" I said over and over.

The moment I could tell he was balanced, I let go. He knew it and leaned to one side, allowing his feet to hit first. He let the bike drop to the ground with a thud and then turned back to look at me.

"You weren't supposed to let go! I told you I would fall!" he screamed.

I jogged to the scene of his abrupt stop, picked up his bike, turned it around and instructed him to get back on.

"What do we do when we fall down? We get back on and try again," I said.

My inspirational words fell flat in the evening air. Visibly disgusted with me (and perhaps even muttering under his breath something about me letting go when I promised I wouldn't), he got back on the bike. He pedaled and found his balance again, yelling at me not to let go this time.

I let go.

He leaned hard to one side, put his feet down, dropped the bike, and turned back to yell at me again. We replayed this mother-son bonding moment over and over until we were both so sick of the whole thing, and we were ready to call it a day. And then out came my husband, twenty minutes after his initial summons, looking like the hero who would teach the disgruntled biker.

They did a few practice runs up and down the street, my husband never letting go of my son's seat. I stood with my arms crossed on the sidewalk, telling myself over and over any success my son had learning to ride his bike came from my initial lessons. I wasn't about to let my husband get all the glory.

After some successful laps up and down the street together, my husband instructed my son he would do the next one alone. My son agreed to the plan and readied himself on the bike. I stood on the sidewalk, wondering if I should capture the moment on video.

My husband held the seat of his bike for a few seconds and then let go. My son pedaled and kept his balance. He was gliding down the street when it dawned on everyone involved that a key component of learning to ride a bike had been left out - steering. He pedaled forward and increased his speed. His instincts froze.

"Turn! Turn! Turn!" My husband and I yelled together. We ran down the street after him in hopes we could catch him.

The next few seconds unraveled in slow motion. My son and his bike smashed into the front of our neighbor's parked pickup truck. He ricocheted off the car and onto the concrete as his bike fell straight to the ground. Remember George of the Jungle, swinging from vine to vine with ease before he planted his entire body into the side of a tree? My son was now George of the concrete jungle, gliding one moment across the concrete like a king, and the next moment slamming into the front of a parked car.

We raced over to make sure he was ok. He was, so we surveyed the car's front bumper for damage.

"Did he dent the bumper? Was that damage from us or was it already there?" my husband frantically whispered.

"How am I supposed to know?" I whispered back. "I'm just glad I didn't film this."

There was no damage, but in a state of panic and embarrassment, we fled the scene, looking over our shoulders as we ran home with a bike and a child in tow.

When we watch our son ride down the street with no training wheels now and see him remember to steer *away from* the parked cars, we laugh at the memory of the crash.

Some days it feels as if I'm riding my own bike through life, feeling free and wild as the wind blows through my hair, and then there's a parked car in front of me. I panic. And even equipped with all the tools necessary from my Father, I still flail forward and crash, forgetting everything I've learned. As an adult, I realize milestones aren't necessarily the new things I try, but instead they are the proverbial parked cars in front of me - the trials, the stalls, the crises, the hurts - that are looking to make me crash. How I maneuver around them is the milestone; remembering my instruction through Scripture, His guiding hand, and His love to carry me on a new path in the face of those hardships is the real achievement and the real growth.

And I always have to remember, even if it feels like there's no one holding my seat steady and balanced as I ride, His hand is always there.

"It is the Lord who goes before you. He will be with you; he will not leave you or forsake you. Do not fear or be dismayed" (Deuteronomy 31:8).

Song: *Leaning On You, Jesus* by Christy Nockels

How's my heart today?

Attitude of gratitude:

Keep going: There are plenty of times in Scripture where someone cries out, wondering why God feels silent and distant. One of those people is Habakkuk. Read the entire book of Habakkuk (it's only three chapters). Notice how in the first part of Chapter 1, Habakkuk is crying out to God, asking why it seems He is inactive. Contrast the complaints of Habakkuk in the beginning of the book to his prayer in Chapter 3. A key to maneuvering through life is the remembrance of who God is, and even if we fall, He's there to pick us up as we try again.

DAY TWENTY-FOUR

When a wave is presents itself in a medium (such as water), the individual particles within that medium are temporarily displaced. After the transfer of energy (creating the wave), the particles go back to their original position.[3]

A panic attack, for me, is like a succession of angry waves surging over my head, energy colliding with particles in an effort to drown me. And when the anxiety subsides, my mind and body are left in a tattered, exhausted depiction of my original position.

I tattooed a wave on my left wrist to remind me of my sometimes-paralyzing anxiety and also to remember Psalm 107:29, "He made the storm be still, and the waves of the sea were hushed."

God is able to calm my raging seas. He's able to tame the violent waves crashing over me. And He's able to reach out and pull me from those dark places. Anxiety is a byproduct of a world ensnared by sin, not an indicator of the depths of my faith. My struggle with anxiety is not a measurement for my dependence on Jesus nor my obedience to Him. It is a system malfunction of a body in a fallen world. And yes, if I'm being honest, sometimes anxiety stems from my inability to release my white-knuckled grip on control. But other times, I feel fully surrendered to the Father and yet the anxiety still seeps into the marrow of my bones and temporarily

---

[3] Tom Henderson, "What is a Wave?", *The Physics Classroom* (2019): https://www.physicsclassroom.com/Class/waves/u10l1b.cfm.

paralyzes me. You can love the Lord with all your heart and all your soul and still suffer from a myriad of mental health issues.

God doesn't love you any less or push you farther away. In fact, He's equipped people around you to walk with you. He's poured grace out. And if we are a people who believe our Savior endured all the pain sin produced, we have to believe when we are filled with anxiety or feel depressed, our God is not distant in those moments - that's when He's holding us closest. His heart aches for His suffering children.

I won't pretend to understand your struggles, because, the truth is, I don't fully understand my own. I'm learning more each day and becoming better equipped through counseling and community to manage, and hopefully one day, overcome anxiety. But this I know for certain, there is no mountain God cannot move, no body of water He cannot part, and no entanglement of the mind He cannot reign victorious. You are not less in the Kingdom for your struggles; instead, through Jesus you will be made whole.

I await a perfect, heavenly body, one free from the onslaught of the crashing waves anxiety brings. I await with hope, remembering this body I'm in now will fail me, but my God never will.

Song: *Three* by Sleeping At Last

How's my heart today?

Attitude of gratitude:

Keep going: For a long time, I kept my anxiety hidden. Finally, burdened by the weight of it, I brought it into the light within community at church. This did not instantly cure my anxiety, but it did provide me a safe place to discuss, pray and work through it. At one point, I also went to counseling, which I loved. One line in Scripture I always think of when anxiety begins to take hold is Lamentations 3:22, "The steadfast love of the Lord never ceases; his mercies never come to an end." Whatever your battle may be, bring it out into the light and ask God to put people around you as you work through it.

DAY TWENTY-FIVE

Meltdowns ensue and tears are usually shed during shower time in our house. For some reason, my children resist with all their might to get clean. And the older they get, the smellier their bodies get.

I'm not often in my kids' bathroom. I go in there to clean it, but I leave it up to them to alert me when they run out of soap or shampoo. One day, I noticed something they failed to tell me – the soap was all gone. My immediate question to myself was, *How in the world did they use a super-sized bottle of soap that fast?* But then I started to get a little disgusted when better questions came to mind, such as, *How long had the soap been gone? How many showers did they take without soap, as they assured me they were clean from head to toe?* I began to imagine the worst, thinking I should send emails to teachers apologizing for the smell of my children. What if, because I'm around them so often, I didn't notice they smelled?

When they arrived home from school that afternoon, I deluged them with questions. "When was the last time you actually used soap?! When did the soap run out?! Why didn't you tell me?! How dirty are you, on a scale of 1 to 10?"

"Don't worry, mom, water makes us clean, too," said one of my boys with confidence. The others nodded in approval and they ran off to play.

Obviously, we have some things we need to discuss in this house. And we're going to start with the fact that water alone does **not** make you clean.

When my kids are asked to get clean, a whole litany of things go on a checklist for them: undress, turn on the water, get in, rinse, clean (with soap!), rinse, get out, towel off, get dressed, gang towel up, throw dirty clothes in the laundry hamper. Something in that list is bound to get passed over. This time, it just happened to be a crucial portion – getting clean.

My day is a giant check list too, and it starts the moment the alarm clock rings. One thing on my list is vital, and yet it so easily can be the first thing I skip if I'm in a rush or tired.

Quiet time with Jesus.

I can't pinpoint why it's so easy to take quiet time off my daily list, but I have some ideas. If my heart isn't in it, or if I can reason there isn't enough time, I'll pass over it to the next item on the agenda. But this vital component of my day changes everything. My quiet time with the Lord is the pivot point of my day. It's the point where I am reminded of His promises, where I'm wrapped in His love, and it's the time of day where I'm free to be alone with my Father. I can ask Him questions. I can cry. I can pray. And He calls me into this time, asking me as His daughter to make time for Him - no matter what. His Son took my place on the cross, yet I can pass over quiet time because I'm too busy. Something about that doesn't seem fair.

I wonder if you've ever struggled with that too. And I wonder what our lives would look like if we saw our time with the Lord every day as necessary as the breath in our lungs, the blood in our veins, and the water and the food we eat for sustenance. Because, sisters, it's just as important as all those things. Time with our Father is the most important thing we can do all day.

And so, I've decided: Other things on my list can be pushed aside or rearranged, but time alone with my Father must be at the top of my daily regimen.

"For God alone my soul waits in silence;
from him comes my salvation
He alone is my rock and my salvation,
my fortress; I shall not be greatly shaken" (Psalm 62:1).

Song: *Yes and Amen* by Housefires

How's my heart today?

Attitude of gratitude:

Keep going: Digging into Scripture can be daunting. While it seems like a natural practice for Christians to be in the Word of God daily, many of us feel overwhelmed by it, whether by the language or the vast amount of information. I recommend you get your daily time with the Lord in by starting with a Bible study. There's also a great book by Jen Wilkin called *Women of the Word: How to Study the Bible with Both Our Hearts and Our Minds*. Finding a study tool to help while you read will create study patterns to last a lifetime, and that will drastically change the way you read and understand Scripture. Read 2 Timothy 3:16-17 as a reminder of how important and life-changing the Word of God is.

DAY TWENTY-SIX

I was feeling a little "grinchy" on the eve of the first big snow Texas had seen in years. Friends grabbed me at school drop-off and excitedly told me about the prospect of snow. Radio show hosts gushed over weather forecasts, and Facebook feeds filled with hopes and wishes of snow. I grumbled under my breath that all this excitement would most likely be met with disappointment in the morning. Everyone was aware the week started with temperatures in the mid-80s, right? And now snow? Bah humbug.

When the sleet started to hit my windowpanes around 9:30 p.m., I called the kids down from their beds.

"This is it! This is all the snow we'll get! Run out and grab some sleet on your tongues and enjoy it while it lasts!"

Their bare feet hit the pavement and didn't even register the cold. Mouths open to the heavens above, they caught bits of rain and sleet with joy in their hearts. I ushered them back into the warmth after a few minutes and re-tucked them into their beds.

About an hour and a half later, I tucked myself into bed. Realizing I had forgotten to take my medicine, I popped up from bed and ran to the kitchen. When I came back, a glimmer caught my eye from the backyard. I looked and saw our trampoline completely covered in white. I yelled for my husband to come see. Part of me wanted to make sure I wasn't imagining it. He resisted for a few minutes, but when he met me at the back door we stood in quiet awe. I then rushed to the front door to make sure it wasn't just the backyard enjoying this snow cover. Indeed, the snow was everywhere.

The next morning the snow gorgeously and delicately covered the tops of roofs, the branches of the still-green trees, and cars. I was captivated by it all. As the sun woke the resting earth and put the snow on further display, I was speechless. I couldn't post any photos to social media because I couldn't wrap my mind fully around what I was in. A winter wonderland surrounded me, a doubter turned full-fledged believer.

That snow wrecked me. It was a good, necessary wrecking; the kind of wrecking that brings about deep heart change. I doubted and sneered at the seemingly impossible. I made God smaller than snow in Texas. And instead of reprimanding my hardened heart, He showered grace and mercy and purity down in the form of snow. He proved me wrong and called me to deeper faith in His abilities.

If I'm going to live in true faith, I have to be wrecked for Jesus first. I have to abandon all the things I think are possible and open my heart to the limitless possibilities the Father holds within His powerful, life-giving hands. I have to wreck the tiny box I've put Him in and give Him the space He truly deserves – which is the entirety of space itself.

When the disciples asked Jesus who would be greatest in the kingdom of heaven, their hearts had not yet been wrecked. They held tight to notions of power and leadership that the world created and did not yet understand the upside-down economy of loving the least and serving others before serving self.

But our Father forgives us when we forget how big He truly is, and He instead comes bearing great gifts, gifts like snow in south Texas. This snow did not slosh and mix with mud but covered and highlighted the magnificent miracle of creation. And in the same way the earth was covered with white, we are covered and washed "whiter than snow" (Psalm 51:7). Praise be to God in the highest.

Song: *Heaven Meets Earth* by All Sons & Daughters

How's my heart today?

Attitude of gratitude:

Keep going: Read Psalm 24. Grab a journal and write the entire psalm. Then write it in your own words. God's ownership of everything He has created is a starting point to understanding His power. In what ways do you tend to make God too small?

DAY TWENTY-SEVEN

Facebook's Timehop can be a fun reminder of the past. I love the photos and videos that pop up to remind me where I was at a moment in time now behind me. I can recall my parenting journey, when life seemed it would forever be full of diapers, bottles and sleepless nights.

And then sometimes my Timehop statuses remind me how far I've come in my faith journey.

Facebook reminded me of a status I wrote years ago, one where I "wanted more Jesus" during a Christmas season. The status gnawed at me all day. It actually gnawed at me for a few days. I went to bed thinking about it and woke up thinking about it. During my quiet time in the book of Acts, it hit me why I couldn't shake the feeling that "wanting more Jesus" just didn't sit right with me.

How can I want more Jesus when I don't even fully know how to live out a life given over to him with the amount of Jesus I already have? If I want *more* Jesus, does that mean I reduce him to nothing more than a cute Christian saying? Am I able to siphon off bits and pieces of Jesus at my own pleasure, taking in only the parts I can handle at a time?

That's when I realized I don't want more Jesus, per se. I don't want Jesus to come and pour Himself into me as a refreshing pick-me-up during busy holiday or parenting seasons. I need to move from passive waiting into active looking. I need to remember when I accepted Jesus as my Savior, He gave me a piece of Himself – the Holy Spirit. I already have all the Jesus I could possibly handle, and to be honest, I'm not fully living out the sacrificial, servant lifestyle loving Him calls me to. I'm living it out in bits and pieces here and there. I don't need more Jesus, because He's already given me all of Himself.

I shouldn't say I want more Jesus. I should say I want to *look* more like Jesus. *Love* more like Jesus. *Serve* more like Jesus.

When Paul visited Athens in Acts 17: 22-27, he looked around and declared, "Men of Athens, I perceive that in every way you are very religious. For as I passed along and observed the objects of your worship, I found also an altar with this inscription: 'To the unknown god.' What therefore you worship as unknown, this I proclaim to you. The God who made the world and everything in it, being Lord of heaven and earth, does not live in temples made by man, nor is he served by human hands, as though he needed anything, since he himself gives to all mankind life and breath and everything. And he made from one man every nation of mankind to live on all the face of the earth, having determined allotted periods and the boundaries of their dwelling place, that they should seek God, and perhaps feel their way toward him and find him. Yet he is actually not far from each one of us."

I don't want to be one of the religious people Paul talked about. I don't want to worship my God in ignorance, forgetting I already have so much more of Him and His love than I deserve. I want to wake up and actively remember He gives to all his children life and breath and **all things**. It is in Him there is even life at all.

I don't want a quick fix of Jesus. I want a life-long, life-changing, life-giving embodiment of Jesus to flood my daily life. I want the kind of heart change that takes comfort and flips it to service. It's time to take the gift He's given me and unwrap it in new and profound ways.

Song: *How Deep the Father's Love for Us* by Austin Stone Worship

How's my heart today?

Attitude of gratitude:

Keep going: Read Isaiah 42. This is a gorgeous prophecy about the coming of Jesus. Read all the qualities written about the Savior who would rescue the world, knowing those promises written are for you too. We can't siphon off more or less of Jesus because He gives us everything. The question then becomes: How will we allow that knowledge to change our lives?

DAY TWENTY-EIGHT

My boys begged me to buy Bean Boozled at the grocery store. I had no idea what it was, but they assured me it was "the most fun jellybean game ever." Thankfully, this uber-fun candy game came in at under $5, so I obliged and purchased it.

Because they are part of the wacky YouTube generation, the boys asked if they could use our GoPro to film while they played the game. They have recorded themselves building LEGOs and opening new Hot Wheels, all in anticipation of posting on a YouTube Channel that doesn't exist. Before recording, I asked the boys to explain to me what Bean Boozled was. They showed me the back of the box and walked me through the premise. There are two jellybeans that look identical but have different tastes. For example, one jellybean could be either spoiled milk or coconut, booger or juicy pear, dead fish or strawberry banana smoothie. You spin the spinner to see which jellybean color you'll be dealt, pop it in your mouth, and see if you've gotten the nasty flavor or the delicious one. They asked if I would like to play, but I graciously opted out. There was no way I would risk putting a jellybean in my mouth that tasted like barf. Nope. Not today. Not ever.

The boys took the game upstairs along with three giant cups of water, bowls (for spitting out the undesired jellybeans) and napkins. We helped them set the GoPro up, and we left them to it. My tech-savvy husband pulled up the feed of their video on his cell phone. After an animated introduction with the instructions to "Smash that subscribe button!," they spun the wheel and began.

After only a few minutes we were laughing so hard we could barely breathe. One by one they would take turns putting jellybeans in their mouth without hesitation. They would make faces and spit out the gross ones, then guzzle water to drown out the taste. And each time, they willingly put their hand in the batch for a new jellybean, knowing full well this one could taste even worse than the last.

This went on for 27 minutes. I initially bet my husband they would wear out after five minutes, but the three of them endured some of the nastiest flavors of jellybeans for almost half an hour. Talk about endurance. Even after experiencing 27 minutes of torture, they still asked if I wanted to join in the fun. My answer remained a steadfast no, but I was grateful for the laughs.

The remaining jellybeans are still sitting in the Bean Boozled box on my kitchen counter. Each time I look at them, I think how grateful I am that I serve a God who isn't trying to Bean Boozle me. I don't have to wake up each day and wondering what God will spin that day; will I end up with a day that tastes like canned dog food, or will I be lucky enough to draw savory chocolate? I don't serve a God of chances. I serve a God who knows all and sees all.

It's right there in the first line of our Bibles: "In the beginning, God created the heavens and the earth" (Genesis 1:1). God knew what He would create, and He created it. In those six days of creation, not once did He experience trial and error. On the seventh day He also chose intentional rest and then called us to join in with him. As time progressed and His most precious creation – humankind – let Him down, He did not falter in His plans. He did not turn His back. He just kept *loving us more*. There is nothing left to chance with a God so mighty and so powerful He would choose grace for people who didn't deserve it.

Rest in that today, sisters. Rest in the truth that the God of the universe isn't playing a big game of Bean Boozled with you, one day spinning a nasty day and the next spinning a glorious one. All of the joys and struggles are seen and known by God. And through them, He does not leave or forsake us (Hebrews 13:5). His plans for you are not haphazardly thrown together with fingers crossed in hopes everything will work out. He is the God of the beginning and the end; whose breath fills your lungs and whose Spirit fills your being. Rest in the truth that your foundation is firm and unwavering, full of abounding grace. And from that abundance of grace, let us give an abundance of thanks.

Song: *How Could I Ask For More* By Christy Nockels

How's my heart today?

Attitude of gratitude:

Keep going: Read Romans 4:13-25. This is one of my favorite discussions on faith by Paul. Paul uses the example of Abraham to convince his readers God is true to His promises. He is exactly who He says He is, and He will always be that way. Which part of this piece of Scripture stands out most to you? Why?

DAY TWENTY-NINE

I think there are secret meetings that go on in my kids' bedrooms before they traverse the stairs and embark upon the day. I imagine they go something like this:

"Guys, today. Today! It's a new day and there are limitless possibilities. What's the consensus on how we tackle today? Delightful and charming or irritating and out of control?"

And then, I imagine the five of them agree on how their behavior for that day will go. And they always agree to go all in together - when you're a band of brothers and sisters, it's all or nothing.

Some days, they opt for delightful and charming, and I'll have an array of handy helpers eager to clean up toys and do homework. But other days, they take an entirely different route.

Color on the walls? You bet. Make sure to pick the color that will stand out the most, though. Biting? Don't leave that one off the list, and to make things even more interesting, let's make sure to bite areas of each other visible to the general public so Mom will get some horrified looks when she drags us to the grocery store. We'll go all out, fighting and tattling on each other, complaining about every option Mom envisions for our day, but we'll let her off easy at bedtime, and say something sweet that melts her heart. Then she'll forget all the trouble we caused. This will be fun.

But it isn't fun for me. The range of emotions I feel at any given point in the day makes me sometimes wonder if I have multiple personalities. How is it possible that this gift - this good and perfect gift - can cause so much struggle?

Motherhood is messy and wonderful at the same time. We have our good days, and we have the days that push us to our knees. There are moments of gratitude, and moments where we wonder how God could have ever chosen us for this life-changing task.

But there's beauty in every bit of break down. Hebrews 4:15-16 states, "For we do not have a high priest who is unable to sympathize with our weaknesses, but one who in every respect has been tempted as we are, yet without sin. Let us then with confidence draw near to the throne of grace, that we may receive mercy and find grace to help in time of need."

Christ came down to live in this imperfect world and suffered the same trials and temptations we do. There's not a single day that goes by our Savior doesn't *feel* what we feel, because He lived it. Give thanks *you are so loved* that Jesus walked the sinful ground so He could feel your sorrow. Understand your pain. Comfort your confusion.

Motherhood is messy, but all you need do is come boldly to the throne of grace to receive what no one can take away from you - mercy and grace…just when you need it most.

Song: *For Your Glory & My Good* by All Sons & Daughters

How's my heart today?

Attitude of gratitude:

Keep going: The testing of my patience with my children always seems to come when things around me are already spiraling out of control. If I pray for more patience, the opportunity to exude it comes when I'm exhausted and stressed, pushing me into reactive mode. Maybe you feel that way too. Read 2 Corinthians 12:9. Write it down somewhere and underline the word "weakness." Circle the word "power." Notice the word "weakness" is used twice, as is the word "power." For each weakness, there is power. In motherhood, I feel my weaknesses are exposed daily and, at times, seem to multiply. God can be glorified in those places if I first surrender my attempt to control them. Make a list of the places you feel weakest in your parenting and then next to each one, write, "but God's power is made perfect in this." God will use your weaknesses to reveal more of Himself to you.

DAY THIRTY

I'm eating pico de gallo as I write this. The fresh peppers, tomatoes, onions and cilantro are piled high on my tortilla chip. This could be my meal for breakfast, lunch and dinner…no questions asked. And now that I think about it, pico has not only satisfied some of my cravings but some of my favorite memories have been forged around a bowl of it.

My snack choice may be an odd tidbit of information to share, but the context helps the situation: I'm a Texas girl, and in Texas, we take pico de gallo serious. And queso. Oh, and guacamole. Those three, when done well (and right!) can give life to any taco night and can equally stand alone as a meal. In Texas, we hold fast and strong to our beliefs about who serves the cheesiest queso, the freshest pico and the most mouth-watering guac. And yes, we'll always pay more to have them added to our meals. Don't even bother asking.

I'm sitting here eating pico and letting the crumbs of my chips fall into my lap, all while thinking about the last thing I want to say in this space we've shared together. And it comes to me like a lightning bolt to the heart – context is important.

Context is important because rambling on about pico de gallo, queso and guacamole might not make much sense if I said I was in Michigan with the snow falling around me. But when I mention I'm deep in the heart of Texas, you're probably imagining me enjoying it with my cowboy boots on, and you wouldn't be too far off.

Context is important for storytelling too, and the most important story we have access to is Scripture.

One context most forgotten about is the context of Scripture. It's easy to get swept away in the feel-good verses penned with gorgeous script and appealing colors. But Scripture isn't about making you feel good temporarily; its purpose is to set you free and radically change your life. It's the story of God Himself, breathed into a book we are undeserving to hold and read. And yet how easy it is to take verses out of context and apply them as best we see fit. I'm guilty of this, using Scripture to fit my circumstances instead of understanding it in the context of who God is and how that does not necessarily change my circumstances but my perspective. Scripture is most effective when we let it remain the supernatural power it is.

I'll never forget a professor in seminary telling our class not every word in Scripture is meant just for us. Scripture is for teaching, rebuking, correcting and training (2 Timothy 3:16), but the Bible as a whole was not written so I could pull verses at my leisure and apply them as I see fit.

Now more than ever the world needs a generation of women who diligently spend time studying God's Word, discerning His voice, and understanding the context of which it was written. We need an active generation of women who will carry this message on and then pass this knowledge and wisdom to younger generations. God doesn't need us, but He chose us. Sisters, arm yourselves with the Word of God in such a way the enemy flees and false teachers shudder. This is our time.

Song: *Great Things* by Phil Wickham

How's my heart today?

Attitude of gratitude:

Keep going: I hope you have felt encouraged over these last 30 days. The goal of each of these "Keep going" sections is to push you further into Scripture. Sister, you have all the tools you need to become a powerful woman of God's Word. Don't let the world fool you into thinking that higher education, social status or financial status have any part of that. It's a lie to deter you away from the truth God has for you. But don't let your time with Him stop here. Find a reading plan or a Bible study and make time with God the ultimate priority in your life. And watch what happens when you spend time with Him and allow His Word to transform you. Keep going.

ACKNOWLEDGEMENTS

I fell in love with Jesus in a whole new way writing this book. He revealed His heart to me with each word.

Jimmy, thank you for making space for me to write. It's no easy feat keeping our brood quiet in the house when I'm writing and editing. You encouraged me over and over to keep writing, never holding it against me when it took up any extra time I had. Thank you for that and for loving me more than I deserve. You lead our family well. I like you and I love you.

Thank you to my five beautiful children who allowed me to share these stories. Thank you for giving me grace as I worked on this book (and every day as a mom). Thank you for cheering the loudest when you saw the book for the first time. You five give me daily glimpses of Jesus' love.

Mom, thank you for letting me call you and bounce ideas around. Thank you for loving me as I changed my mind a million times, backed out of the project on several occasions and when I finally succumbed to obedience in finishing. Thank you for cheering me on and praying for this book. And thanks for putting up with me all these years. I'm so thankful to call you mom.

Dad, thank you for teaching me how to work hard and love extravagantly. We may never cheer for the same college team, but I'm sure glad we are on the same family team. I'm so thankful to be your daughter.

To the teachers at SonKids Christian Preschool and Kindergarten, thank you for allowing me to write devotionals for you. Thank you for the hugs in the hallways and the life you poured into me. This book is just as much yours as it is mine.

Jamie, Jessy, Amber and Rachel, thank you for praying me through – everything.

And to my WoodsEdge staff family, thank you for praying over this book and getting excited about it. Even though I was only part of your team for a few weeks, you wrapped me in your arms and loved me big. I love serving Jesus with you.

KEEP GOING

ABOUT THE AUTHOR

Jessica Fraser is a former CEO who found her calling working for her local church. She is a wife and mother of five who currently resides in Texas. You can follow her on Instagram @jessica_fraser.